One Hundred Hearts

Inspiring Stories from the Women who Lived Them

TERRY SIDFORD

BALBOA.
PRESS

A DIVISION OF HAY HOUSE

Balboa Press books may be ordered through
booksellers or by contacting:

Balboa Press
A Division of Hay House
1663 Liberty Drive
Bloomington, IN 47403
www.balboapress.com
1 (877) 407-4847

Because of the dynamic nature of the Internet, any web addresses or
links contained in this book may have changed since publication and
may no longer be valid. The views expressed in this work are solely those
of the author and do not necessarily reflect the views of the publisher,
and the publisher hereby disclaims any responsibility for them.

The author of this book does not dispense medical advice or prescribe
the use of any technique as a form of treatment for physical, emotional,
or medical problems without the advice of a physician, either directly
or indirectly. The intent of the author is only to offer information
of a general nature to help you in your quest for emotional and
spiritual well-being. In the event you use any of the information in
this book for yourself, which is your constitutional right, the author
and the publisher assume no responsibility for your actions.

Any people depicted in stock imagery provided by Thinkstock are
models, and such images are being used for illustrative purposes only.
Certain stock imagery © Thinkstock.

Print information available on the last page.

ISBN: 978-1-5043-3763-2 (sc)
ISBN: 978-1-5043-3764-9 (e)

Library of Congress Control Number: 2015911962

Balboa Press rev. date: 08/13/2015

Contents

Acknowledgments

Many thanks to Annette Velarde and Stacy Dymalski for partnering with me on my amazing journey of writing this book. Your love, spirit, and belief in this project helped keep me going and made this book possible.

And of course, thank you to the 100 courageous women who filled out the surveys and shared their stories. In my lifetime, I've had the tremendous honor to work with and know some pretty incredible women, including my mother, grandmother, sister, and many wonderful friends and clients. I would not be where I am today without each and every one of you.

With love,
Terry

Dedication

This book is dedicated to my loving family and friends, starting with my parents, who both endured challenges, but never forgot who they were, or lost their ability to love their children unconditionally.

To my father who is a loving, intelligent, funny, adventurous, deep thinker, as well as an inspirational leader who loves life. Your ability to stay in touch with our family is an enduring quality that I will never take for granted. Thank you for always showing who you are and not being afraid to be emotional.

To my mother, who is an example of grace, love, strength, tenderness, strong will, beauty and intelligence. You had your own life challenges that you courageously conquered. In spite of those challenges, your love for your family has been strong, deep, and constant. But as I got older I was able to understand the depth of your circumstances and how you came out stronger, but without losing yourself. You are an example to women everywhere.

To my loving husband, who is always there for me unconditionally. You see the best in me and your enduring love keeps me going. Thank you also for being a positive influence in my sons' lives, as well as a wonderful example of spirituality, optimism, and living life to the fullest.

To my two amazing sons, who taught me how to be a better person. Your love, intelligence, humor and adventure for living are truly inspiring. I'm so proud that you have both grown up to be responsible adults who make a difference in the world.

To my sons' father, Mark, who worked with me after we were divorced to raise our sons. You helped shape them into the loving adults they are today.

To my two brothers, who have the biggest hearts on the planet. You both have been there for me every step of the way. I am so lucky to know such wonderful men and to feel your love and connection.

To my sister, another amazing example of heart and courage. You raised six children while getting your master's degree, all while working outside the home. You had many reasons to quit along the way, but you NEVER gave up. You amaze me daily.

To my dear friends and coaching clients, old and new. Thank you for your lifelong friendships and sisterhood. You show me daily how to live life fully with a courageous heart.

And lastly, I dedicate this book to "Rosa" (you know who you are). You are the inspiration for this book. And to the 100 women who were courageous enough to fill out the surveys that are the backbone of this book. Even though collectively we have 100 hearts, together as women we share just one.

Forward

It is hard to find words for how much I love Terry Sidford's *One Hundred Hearts*; not just the stories, but also the process it took to create such an insightful book. I believe every woman should have an opportunity to delve into these stories, as they are reflections of the lives of all women. Not only is this book an inspiration, it's also a wonderful guide for men, specifically husbands, fathers, and sons. The more clearly men understand our voices, the more clearly they will champion the change needed to honor all women of the world.

The benefaction of a woman (and their work as mothers, partners, wives, co-workers, etc.) is so incredibly undervalued, not only by men, but sadly by other women, as well. The contributions and courage a woman gives is beyond measure. The legacy most women leave is arduously giving to everyone, but not to themselves. Pressured to be perfect, to please everyone, to nurture everyone, we forget about our needs. It is not until most of us hit our late thirties to forties that we truly begin to seek and honor our truths and natural gifts.

One Hundred Hearts has flawlessly captured these truths we hold within and reminds us that we need to champion every woman everyday. Encourage women, invest in them, and most of all encourage them to invest in themselves. Remember the stories in *One Hundred*

Hearts and dig deep with those around you...they may be yearning for *you* to hear the stories of *their* hearts.

Kristina Plunta – Founding partner of PUREfourhundred and author of *Queens & Princesses: A Mother and Daughter's Reflections on Relationships, Self-Discovery and Love*

Introduction

Courage doesn't always roar.
Sometimes courage is the little voice
at the end of the day that says,
I'll try again tomorrow.
—Mary Anne Radmacher

Every woman's life is unique, but every woman's heart beats with courage. *One Hundred Hearts* is a collection of short stories that tell of the events in real women's lives, when courage sometimes roars, but other times only whispers the encouragement needed to just get through another day. Some of the stories are so easily identifiable that they'll literally bring you to tears; while others touch your heart in ways you never imagined or expected. In all cases, they inspire, uplift, and reflect your own courage, no matter how hard it's been for you to see courage in yourself.

The seed of my idea for this book took root when I thought back to my own childhood. I had to overcome many challenges growing up and remember a defining moment when I lost everything material due to a con-artist boyfriend. I had no money, home, car, or job. I was sleeping on my friend's couch. I hit rock-bottom and knew I had a choice to survive or not. In that moment, *something* gave me the gift of knowing I had the strength inside to overcome anything. No one could take away my spirit. That realization gave me power—power that until then, I never knew I had. I picked myself up and felt happy that I now knew I could handle anything in life because I would always be able to rely on myself. Just to know that is a gift.

In addition to my own story, I saw courage in my mother, sister, grandmother, and other women whom I got to know. In my 15 years of life coaching, I have had the tremendous honor of peering into women's souls and witnessing their undeniable courage to never completely give up in the face of hardship, loss, and divorce. Each and every one of them has been an inspiration to me. And just when I thought I had witnessed every kind of human courage possible, I personally experienced seeing my friend lose her young, talented, loving son. This woman showed the ultimate display of courage, grace, and love in the face of any mother's worst nightmare. I was so moved by her ability to get out of bed in the morning, knowing that she had to face yet another day without her son, that I wanted to tell her story. I believe it will help other women realize that they too are capable of pressing on even when the unthinkable relentlessly stares them in the face.

I know every woman has her own story of courage, and I wanted to write a book that illustrates a few of those stories and then share them with the world. To begin, I created a survey asking questions about heart and courage to see if I could coax out a few personal tales. It took me over a year to gather 100 surveys, but every one of them moved me deeply. Based on the survey, I crafted a compilation of women's stories that illustrate a woman's courage is something to be honored and celebrated, not hidden or avoided, and help us feel the common bonds that we all share as women. Each chapter poses one of the survey questions, followed by a short story that illustrates the essence of the responses collectively, and then the actual verbatim answers to all survey questions are listed at the end of this book. It's my way of using characters and situations to transform the data into moving, personal stories that I think we can all relate to in one way or another. In any case, you will feel the common bonds that we all share as women when you read these experiences.

The surveys confirmed what I already knew: women are multifaceted and have an ability to make significant changes for the better in this world. However, most of the time they don't realize it, mainly because they put so much pressure on themselves to do it all, and do it perfectly. Most women do not know how incredible they are and how much they contribute to everyone around them. Many of the women I surveyed were surprised when they realized how courageous they are in their lives. This survey was like a mirror for their courage that many of them had never looked into until they began to write their responses.

Enjoy reading these stories, and may they inspire you and all the women in your life to live a more courageous, loving, authentic life.

With love and gratitude,
Terry Sidford

P.S. In case you're wondering how *you* would respond to these questions, the survey is on my website (*www.createyourlifecoaching.net*) for anyone to take.

1

How Do You Define Courage?

Courage is being true to myself and standing by my heart.
—Summary answer from 100 women's surveys

While reading the responses to this question from 100 women, two themes emerged as the overwhelming consensus:

1. Courage is being true to who you are, no matter what the circumstances are in life.
2. Courage is facing your fears.

I have observed that people often morph into what society, family, or friends want them to be. As such, standing up for who you are is one of the most courageous acts in the world. This is particularly true for women who, over the centuries, have been forced to play small in order to hide their true greatness.

Facing fears is not the same thing as not *feeling* fear. Almost unanimously, the 100 women surveyed for the book wrote that the courageous act was moving forward *in spite* of their fears, all while feeling the emotions associated with being afraid. They also said that facing fear gives them the ability to dig deep and connect to their inner strength they otherwise may not have known was there.

Most of the time, we think courage is a big emotion we muster up in times of need, when the clouds descend and life collapses around us with loud booming noises. But I have often found just the opposite to be true. Sometimes it is the quietest of moments, when I can barely hear my heart speaking to me, that require the most courage. It is in these moments of deep reflection that I have been gifted a new, clearer lens through which to see myself. But once I peer through it, there is no turning back—marching forward with my courage pressing me on is the only thing possible.

> *If you don't design your own life plan, chances*
> *are you'll fall into someone else's plan. And guess*
> *what they have planned for you? Not much.*
> —Jim Rohn

Martina's Story

Martina looked around her, pausing to focus on each item in her all-too-familiar room. It suddenly struck her how beige everything was. The color of the comfortable sofa and loveseat had been labeled Golden Fields when she had ordered them from the local furniture superstore some five years prior. The paint on the walls was Harvest

Warmth, trimmed in white. The coffee and end tables were Honey Oak. Even the throw pillows were a crosshatch of browns.

She smiled to herself when she spotted her daughter's secret stash of books hidden behind the fireplace tools. The daisies she'd bought yesterday shone like neon from the middle of the coffee table. Everything matched. Everything was *perfect*. She glanced at her watch and made note that she'd been sitting in the same place for four hours—her spot at one end of the sofa. She moved the cushions around often so her position didn't become permanently dented or worn. The TV remote, her laptop, and the latest issue of *People* magazine were neatly placed on the end table near her. Two more hours until Cole and Savannah came home from school. Two more hours that she was free to do whatever she wanted, if only she knew what that was.

This restlessness had been getting to her for almost a year, ever since Max started first grade. Weekdays were the worst. The weekends, when everyone was home and she had plenty of things to do, were better. It was the hours between cleaning the house after the kids had left in the morning and waiting for them to get home that could pull her into the darkness. Martina fidgeted. She picked up the remote and surfed through the afternoon talk shows, but nothing caught her interest. She was too distracted by the conversation that seemed to be going on in the back of her mind, almost without her. Once again the anxiety spoke to her, telling her to think about things that didn't need to take center stage.

Maybe she should have another baby. Cole was just six, Savannah 10, and she knew of plenty of women who got pregnant after 35. Tina Fey, Celine Dion, Brooke Shields: they all had kids after 40, and look at them—they were still hot, and their kids were just fine. Not one Down Syndrome in the whole bunch. But oh my God, babies were so much work, and the extra pregnancy weight had been *really* hard to take off after Cole. Besides, another baby felt like putting off the inevitable, like trying to move backward rather than forward.

Martina let her thoughts float. Maybe a job would give her direction, grounding. She hadn't worked since Savannah had been born. Maybe she could get something part time, but where? She mentally made a quick list of the possibilities. Given that she had been out of the workforce for so long, she knew she'd descended to employment footing equal to that of high school graduates. She felt she couldn't bear the gossip that would ensue if she took a job at Starbucks or Whole Foods. She knew exactly what women would be saying behind her back. *Do you think Max has lost his job? She can't be making more than minimum wage there. What's she thinking? I thought she said she had a college degree. Why would she be spending her days doing that if she* really *has a degree?*

Martina's bachelor's degree in Italian had meant something in the working world when she'd graduated. Because of it, she had landed a job with American Express, answering calls from their Italian-speaking clientele. That's how she'd met Max; he'd worked in the same department. Both of them had left the company three

4

years after they'd married. Max went on to work for Wells Fargo's credit card division, and she'd taken a part-time job with a small magazine publisher, doing office work.

Two years later, when Savannah was born, both Martina and Max thought it would be best if Martina focused on their family while Max concentrated on his career and provided income. To her surprise, Martina found she loved being home with her daughter and was fully prepared for her son, Cole, when he was born four years later. Her full schedule of childcare, play dates, PTO, Sunday school, and superficial friendships with women in the same situation filled Martina's life with so much activity she didn't notice that Max wasn't home much. When Cole started first grade the previous September, Martina thought the extra time in her day would be snapped up with finally getting the house really clean and organized, grocery shopping, and making fancy dinners. Oh, and maybe even getting a run in before the kids came home.

Presently, the house was clean. The laundry was done. Dinner was in the Crock-Pot. It was raining outside, so a run was deleted from her to-do list. No, Marina finally admitted to herself. Her problem was that it was raining *inside*.

Life seemed to be trying to turn pages Martina wasn't ready for. She often felt lonely, like she had lost herself somewhere along the way and was left without a compass. She loved her kids madly, but knew they could not always be the center of her life. They would grow up and move away. Max and she had a stable, pleasant relationship, although somewhere between breast-feeding and control-top panties, Martina's fire for her husband had begun sputtering. Max seemed to be fulfilled with his career in banking and never gave any indication that he would ever want anything more than what they had. He was content, probably even happy. Max was a good guy; he wasn't the problem. The problem was the cloud front that moved into Martina's soul during those long, quiet afternoons she spent planted on the couch. This was something fundamental, something bone-deep. It scared her to listen to the conversation inside her head: *What are you doing with your life? Whatever happened to the young woman who was going to travel Europe, drink wine, and experience men? You've become the one thing you never thought you would—average, typical, unseen, and unheard.*

Martina was certain her sad opinion of herself was useless. It wasn't any more significant than any of her other dead-end opinions.

Martina looked around her beige living room again. There was no getting around it. *She* was beige. She blended into a life she'd crafted with her own hands—an existence that had ended up being merely the backdrop for her children's and husband's lives. Step by step, moment by moment, she had created a life that was expressed through others. She lived vicariously through her children, but rarely personally reveled in her own existence. Everything matched. Everything was perfect. Everything was safe. Nothing about it was meaningful. None of it was an expression of Martina, a woman whose dreams and hopes and joys and sorrows had been set aside while she checked off her to-do list. Her life was the Denny's menu, replete with photos of how beautiful it all appeared, but she never got to relish the full, real flavor of the meal.

She still had an hour before the kids had to be picked up at school. She needed to do something, anything, that would tell her if there was a shred of the pre-family Martina left. The idea that there was just enough time to go buy something red or lime or purple flew into her head. She jumped from her spot, and uncertain fingers picked up her purse. She paused. Between her fingers, she thought she could feel the very end of the string that was tied to her being. For the first time ever, she courageously interrupted the conversation in the back of her mind. She would be her own superhero. *Don't worry. I've got you, and I'm not letting go.*

TJ Maxx was its usual madhouse of women in search of that perfect bargain, whatever that was. Martina pulled down on her blazer to straighten it and clutched her purse tighter under her arm. She was on a mission. There was an item somewhere in here just waiting for her, something important that she needed, *for sure*. Not like all the other women in the store looking for something they thought they needed; there was some *Thing* the Universe had placed in here specifically for Martina, specifically for this moment.

Taking a deep breath and hoping she wouldn't run into anyone she knew, Martina marched into the racks of clothes. As she thumbed through the size medium tops, there was nothing that didn't remind her of beige. Certain that slacks of any kind could not be the Thing, she moved to the dresses. Long, short, backless, lace, skimpy, *blah, blah, blah*. She looked at each and every one, but none was the Thing.

She moved on to the lingerie, the shoes, the scarves, the purses, the jewelry—nothing. Glancing at her watch, she began to doubt her previous decision about not needing a doctor: the kids expected her to be waiting for them in the pick-up line in only 15 minutes, and she was rummaging through a discount store looking for some Thing her angels had left for her. Maybe she was crazy after all.

Deflated, Martina decided to make one last-ditch effort in the household items aisles. There was a shiny silver paperweight—a heavy heart, perhaps? The plates with birds in flight? Yuck. So cliché. She headed to the *nobody-else-in-the-world-wants-this-stuff* markdown aisle. Notecards? No. Scented candle? They give her headaches. Ironing board cover? Do they really still make those? Miniature globe ...? *Oh my God, stop!* A globe the size of softball was sitting behind boxes of shot glasses. Martina had to stand tiptoe on the bottom shelf in order to reach it. It was cheap, almost weightless in the palm of her hand. It had not been updated since 2000. Martina knew this because the Panama Canal was labeled as U.S. territory. How she knew this, she wasn't sure, but she gave herself a pat on the back for being such a geography buff. She rotated it, thinking of the child in Asia who had glued this map onto a cardboard ball so long ago. Holding it in her palm, she imagined the journey it had needed to travel to end up on this steel shelf, waiting for her.

Suddenly, Italy was staring her in the face. Italy (with Rome and Naples and Venice and Florence) was asking why she'd never come. Long ago she had pledged her love to Italy and all she believed it to be, but had never gone to see it for herself. Martina had found the Thing. She'd figure out later exactly what the Universe was trying to tell her through this globe, and she zoomed toward the front of the store.

Her heart sank when she got to the checkout line. What had she expected? There were at least 15 people in front of her, only three cashiers, and she had a mere 10 minutes to get to the school. She started to leave the globe on one of the shelves that corralled the line of waiting people, but she could not bring herself to do it. She felt as though that globe was the necessary anchor affixed to the string that tethered her being to this world. Without it the clouds would sweep her away, and it would rain in her soul forever. She then did something that would have never occurred to her before: she allowed herself to be important. Clutching at her purse and the globe, she turned and marched up to a manager-looking sort of person who was observing the cashiers.

"Excuse me. I need to go pick up my kids at school in 10 minutes, so I need to pay for this right now. Can you help me?" Martina heard the words march out her mouth and straight into the manager's ears. She felt as though she'd just made the most ridiculously self-centered demand she'd ever heard in her life. The voice in her head rattled off the possible answers: *You should have planned your time better. What makes you think everyone in that line doesn't have someplace they need to be? You want to buy a two-dollar item, and you think I'm going to make an exception for you?*

Martina waited the eternity it seemed to take for the manager to respond.

"Sure," the manager said as he turned and motioned for Martina to follow him to the end register. Martina's sense of gratitude was enormous. She loved the angels that had whispered in the manager's ear. She loved the manager. She loved all the people standing in line who looked like they could not care less that she had cut in front of them all. She loved her globe.

On time and with a smile that refused to leave her face, Martina spotted Cole and Savannah waiting for her on the corner. The other cars seemed to part just for her, and she swerved her now sleek and elegant minivan up to the curb, hitting the button that opened the side door.

"Ciao, miei bei bambini!" leapt out of Martina's mouth on the wings of joy. Cole and Savannah's jaws dropped, and they stood motionless for a full two counts before tumbling into the back seat.

"You speak another language? What is it?" Savannah exclaimed.

"Where'd you learn it?" Cole chimed in.

"Oh, *miei bambini*! The things you don't know about me. I am so much cooler than you could possibly imagine." Martina smiled as she pulled out into traffic and down familiar streets seen with new eyes.

2

Have You Had the Opportunity to Demonstrate Courage?

For the first time, I stood up for myself.
—Summary answer from 100 women's surveys

There wasn't one survey that did not have an incredibly moving answer to this question. Everyone spoke from the heart. Whether it was family, career, or health, each and every respondent had experienced having to dig deep to keep moving ahead. Most of time they would continue to take care of their loved ones even while they battled some of the most difficult challenges in their lives. One of the common themes was surviving a serious health issue such as breast cancer. I think learning that you have a life-threatening illness and being forced to face the very real possibility that you may not survive is the ultimate challenge to one's courage. Many women in the survey have faced this in their lives but found the courage to survive the process of recovery. All I can say is that I am in awe.

> *"Learn from yesterday, live for today, hope for tomorrow."*—Albert Einstein

Jeanine's Story

"Jeanine? Jeanine! Try to stay with me here. I know this is hard, but you need to listen to what I'm telling you. There will be plenty of time for reflection later."

Jeanine gazed right at Dr. Parsons, but he knew she was looking through him. Jeanine glanced at her husband, John. He was staring wide-eyed at her and reached out to touch her elbow.

"Come on, honey. You can do this," John murmured, as though he was encouraging her to run a marathon. "Let's finish up here, and then we can talk as long as you need to." They both turned back to Dr. Parsons sitting behind his massive mahogany desk. A bookshelf covered the entire wall behind him and was filled with hundreds of medical volumes. Jeanine's eyes wandered across the titles when she suddenly felt John's hand on her elbow again, directing her back to the doctor she had met just two days ago.

"As I was saying, the biopsy confirms stage two breast cancer. Although breast cancer is never good news, stage two is. Today the survival rate for stage two is very high." Dr. Parsons paused and gave a practiced smile to John and Jeanine. She suspected that this was a highly choreographed script he delivered several times a week.

"How many stages are there?" Jeanine cautiously asked.

"There are four, each one determined by the size of the tumor," he patiently replied, never dropping that smile. "Your tumor is a Stage 2B invasive globular, three centimeters in size. When I perform your surgery, if I find cancer cells larger than 0.2 millimeters, but not larger than 2 millimeters, in one to three axillary lymph nodes or to the lymph nodes near the breastbone, I'll need to advance your diagnosis to Stage 3A. I think we caught this very early, so I don't think that will be the case."

"So two should be pretty easy to treat, right?" asked John. Jeanine bristled at his question. This was *her* cancer, and he was already diminishing the seriousness of it.

Dr. Parson's shot John a *you're-going-to-pay-for-that one-buddy* look. He continued. "I've scheduled you for surgery a week from tomorrow. Following that, you will have chemo over a three-month period, followed by five weeks of radiation. Before you leave today, my staff will give you a file of information that addresses each of these procedures in detail. Any questions?"

From the way his voice had lilted upward at the end of the word *questions*, Jeanine knew some kind of response from her was expected, but Jeanine could not seem to think of any. She had just been told that she had cancer, that she would be losing both of her breasts in eight days, and that the next five months were going to be hell. Surely there was something Jeanine was unclear about, but her brain felt like it had turned to oatmeal, and she could not produce a coherent thought. Finally, John leaned forward.

"Why do you have to remove both breasts if there's only cancer in one?"

13

This time, Jeanine could not hold her tongue. "Seriously? You're worried about your squeezebox when *my* life is on the line?"

John's jaw dropped. Dr. Parson's intervened, knowing this argument could take place later without him. He was a doctor after all, not a marriage counselor. "It's a fair question, Jeanine, regardless of the reason it's asked. We've found that when cancer is in one breast, it's almost certainly a ticking time bomb in the other. We take both to make sure you never have to go through this again."

John's eyes filled with tears. "Honey, honestly, I didn't ask because I was worried about *me* ..."

Jeanine moved on without so much as looking at John. "Exactly what is the survival rate for stage two?" she asked, her voice quivering.

"The national statistics for the five-year survival rate are included in your information packet, but it's over 90 percent if we act quickly," Dr. Parsons replied in a tone that implied this number should assuage Jeanine's fears. Jeanine immediately wondered how many died in the sixth year.

"I know you'll think of questions later," Dr. Parsons continued. "Please feel free to send me an e-mail through our clinic website. We'll get back to you within 24 hours." With that the good doctor stood and came around the desk. "I understand that it's hard not to worry, but your prognosis is very, very good," he said has he extended his hand to Jeanine. She stared at it, unsure of what the gesture meant. Was he congratulating her for something? Was he wishing her well? Had they just concluded a negotiation of some kind? John reached over Jeanine and shook the doctor's hand.

"Thank you, Dr. Parsons. Thank you very much," said John in his business voice.

Dr. Parsons left the office. John and Jeanine sat in silence looking at their hands folded in their laps. Jeanine's whole body shivered like it was 15 below zero, but her hands and underarms were sweating profusely. She kept thinking, *I have cancer. I could die*, over and over, as if repeating it would make it believable to her. John was silently crying, lost in his own dreadful imaginings of how he could not raise their children without her. Within 15 seconds a nurse came through the door with a folder. On the cover was a photographic collage of smiling women.

"Hi, Mr. and Mrs. Christianson. My name is Shirley, and I'm Dr. Parson's patient care manager. We've put together this file of information that you'll find very helpful. Please read through it thoroughly before you come back next week. If you have any questions, just give us a call at the number right there or send us an e-mail through the clinic's website, *www.womensoncologycenter.com*." She rattled off the website name like she was filming a commercial. "Now, don't you worry. Dr. Parsons is the best oncologist in the whole city. We'll take very good care of you and have you back to your normal life just as quickly as possible."

Jeanine took the folder from Shirley's hand and gazed into the faces of the women on its cover. "Did all these women have breast cancer?" Jeanine knew it was a stupid question, but it was out of her mouth and hanging heavily in the air for the two beats of silence that followed.

"Uh, you know, I'm really not sure. These folders are given to us by our Temoxifen sales rep as promo items." Again two beats of silence—which seemed like an eternity.

Jeanine looked down at the pictures again. "Oh. Okay," was all she could muster up. She turned to leave, and John told Shirley thank you. John took her hand and held it as they silently wound their way through the serpentine corridors of the hospital to the parking garage. Once they were in the car, they again sat in silence. When John finally turned so he could look at Jeanine, there were tears in his eyes, which unleashed the torrents that had been building up in hers. Ten minutes passed as they held each other and wept.

Finally, John sat up and took Jeanine's face in his hands. "Look at me. We are going to beat this together." Ah, the proverbial coach had entered the car. "We've been through some really tough things, and this is just one more. I'll be with you every step of the way and will do whatever you need. Okay?"

John's tenderness always moved her, always reminded her of why she loved him so much. Even when they were dating 20 years prior, he had been far more kind, far more sensitive than she.

"Okay," Jeanine agreed. "And I'll try really hard to not let this consume me." John had found her hypersensitive mood swings through menstrual cycles, pregnancy, and perimenopause to be almost unbearable, so he knew what

Jeanine was referring to. "I know everything is going to be fine. The next six months will be rocky, but then we can get back to normal. Let's go get ice cream. And a vodka tonic." John let out a sigh of relief, smiled, and turned the car key in the ignition.

For the next week Jeanine poured over the information in the folder, and then on the Internet. She found support groups and blogs and medical websites that talked about nothing but breast cancer. Even among her friends, unbeknownst to her, several of them had battled cancer, and therefore called to offer their encouragement. It seemed to her that breast cancer had touched everyone's life in one way or another; however, she wasn't brave enough to post her condition on her Facebook page. It was too personal for people who barely knew her to know she was losing her breasts. And Jeanine was still not able to articulate it in a way that didn't seem like she was talking about someone else. She spent hours in introspection, but her emotional defenses kept the possibility of death, or worse, painful illness, at arm's length.

The toughest part was telling their kids. Their daughter, Stephanie, was 18 and their son, Marcus, was 15. Each of them had friends who had lost their mothers to breast cancer, and it took a long time to convince them that stage two had a very good recovery rate. During that heart-wrenching evening, Stephanie gave Jeanine a dose of reality.

"Mom, what's with all these percentages? Twenty percent, 40 percent, 90 percent—they don't mean crap, because if it happens to you, it's 100 percent, and that sucks."

She was right. None of the statistics Jeanine found during her research promised that she would be okay. One in eight women is diagnosed with breast cancer at some time in their lives, and it did not comfort her in the least that she was taking the hit for seven other women. Jeanine had done everything right, but was still getting screwed. She had gotten her check-up every year. She bought organic. She did yoga. She took vitamins by the handful. She never smoked and drank only red wine occasionally. Her reward for all that effort was that she was at the mercy of her body's whims, and it had betrayed her. This was *not fair*.

For the first time that week, anger reared its ugly head. Jeanine suddenly felt compelled to yell, to break things, to fling obscenities and blame. Her family knew that look on her face all too well and waited, dreading what was about to come. Looking in their eyes, their fear of her temper slapped her across the face. Jeanine realized her tornado-like outbursts were something they had been forced to put up with all these years, and just like her illness, it wasn't fair. Instead of flying into a rage, Jeanine crumpled into tears, soon joined by the other three people in her family.

A week later, Jeanine woke up in a recovery room to the loving faces of her kids and husband. Her chest was numb and limbs weak. She had faded in and out of sleep throughout the night, only waking when nurses came in to change her IV or empty her drainage bags. It seemed

Jeanine had tubes coming out of her in every direction. The next morning, Dr. Parsons came in and stood at the foot of her bed to talk to John and her about how the procedure went.

"I think we got all of it, but the chemo and radiation will destroy anything that may have been left. Nothing has spread to your lymph nodes, which is the most important thing. We'll give you a month for your incisions to heal before we start chemo. Any questions?"

John and Jeanine glanced at each other and smiled. A *matter-of-factly* delivered "any questions?" had become their inside joke. They had been prepared by all the advice they received from survivors that cancer treatment was a giant, multi-trillion dollar business with hundreds of thousands of customers every year. It would be entirely up to them to make it personal.

"When can I go home?" was Jeanine's only concern.

"We want to monitor you for another day or two. If everything goes well, I'll give you the green light by this weekend," smiled Dr. Parsons.

The next morning Jeanine felt much better. She still had not looked at her chest in a mirror. She decided to wait until she was in the privacy of her own bathroom at home. She had two roommates in the hospital who, like her, had not felt sociable enough to draw their curtains back. There were three beds in the room. Jeanine's was the last one, so she hadn't seen anyone who had come in to visit the other patients. When the nurse came in to check on her that morning, Jeanine asked her about the other two women. "Maybe they'd like to visit for a while?"

"Let me ask them and see how they feel," the nurse said as she poked her head through the curtain next to Jeanine. "Diane, how are you feeling? Think you'd like some company?"

"That's a great idea," said Diane. "Can you help me sit up?"

"Sure. There you go," said the nurse.

The nurse went down the row to the last bed. "Betty, you want to join the party?" Silence. "That's okay. Maybe later."

The nurse drew back the curtain, and Jeanine was stunned. Diane couldn't have been more than 25 years old. From what Jeanine had read, Diane had drawn the short straw from among 250 other women. Diane had a wild mop of curly blonde hair that she pulled back into a loose ponytail. Her eyes were such a deep brown that they were almost black, and her features so delicate she almost looked like a child. Jeanine wondered if she had ever been that pretty in her youth. Then her eyes did what Jeanine dreaded everyone's eyes would do to her— they fell to Diane's chest, where the hospital gown hung completely flat.

"Yup, they took 'em both," she said with disappointment while rolling her eyes.

Jeanine blushed. She was so ashamed that she was even curious, let alone making it so obvious that it was the first thing she wanted to know.

"I'm so sorry. They took both of mine too. How are you feeling?" Jeanine said weakly.

"Well, better than I thought I would. This all happened so fast that I really haven't had time to process it," Diane said chattily. "They told me that I have stage four metastasized breast cancer just two days ago, and now here I am with no tits. Believe me, one week ago when I went in for my checkup at the student health center, this is the last thing I thought would be happening."

Jeanine's jaw dropped. "Stage four? Oh my god, I'm so sorry," Jeanine apologized again, the second time in as many sentences. She was grateful that Diane seemed willing to lead the conversation.

"I know, right? Who thinks about getting breast cancer with they're young? This was the first time I'd ever gone to the doctor for a female exam, and I only went because my friend was going, and it was free. My mom died of breast cancer, but she was, like 40 or something. I think one of my aunts died of it too, but I never knew her. I'm totally dreading my dad getting here. He's going to be a total mess."

Jeanine now knew what she must have sounded like the past week, talking about this awful disease like it had happened to someone else. Her own daughter was only two years younger than Diane, but Jeanine had made sure she had annual exams since she started menstruation at 13. When Jeanine heard about Diane's mother, she felt an anxiety-filled urgency to have Stephanie checked again right away.

"When do you start chemo?" Jeanine asked.

"They haven't told me exactly when yet, but they did say I'd be here for like a month or something. So I guess they'll start that pretty soon. It's going to totally mess up my semester, but my roommate is telling all my professors. Hopefully they'll understand and let me catch up when I get back." Jeanine's heart was sobbing, thinking about how much of her life had laid ahead of her at Diane's age. Would Diane ever finish school? Have her first job? A husband or family?

"I'm feeling so good, it's hard for me to get that anything is really wrong. Maybe it's really the chemo that makes people feel crappy. I guess I'll just have to find out. But I, like, somehow know that this is going to turn out fine. I really do think everything happens for a reason and teaches me something about myself that I'd never be able to learn any other way." Her silver-lining attitude was starting to make Jeanine uncomfortable. She was berating herself for being so morbid. Diane's diagnosis was so much worse than hers, but her thoughts so much brighter. "I'm only worried about my dad. He never really got over losing my mom, and I'm his only child. I've got great friends though. They'll help me take care of him. So ... how are you feeling?"

Thankfully, John and the kids came in just at that moment. Jeanine introduced them to Diane, and then the nurse came in and drew the curtain again, telling Diane that she'd better get some rest. Jeanine's family stayed until she fell back to sleep, which wasn't long. When Jeanine woke up, she laid still for a long time, thinking deeply.

So much of life is out of our control, so much of it a game of chance, she thought. Jeanine had lived her life chasing control, trying desperately to be the captain of her ship. When events occurred unexpectedly, or people didn't do what she thought they should, Jeanine was judgmental, angry that things weren't going according to her plan. She had been lucky enough to marry a man who wanted to be a good husband and a father. She had never had to deal with familial problems like alcohol or drugs or unemployment. Her kids were responsible, kind people. Jeanine had lived a full life that included a good education, loyal friends, and more good times than bad.

Diane had lived none of that.

It wasn't right, it wasn't fair, and there was nothing to be done about it. Jeanine realized that if she continued resenting her cancer, feeling cheated or victimized, an emotional cancer would grow in her heart that would also afflict everyone in her life. *What an amazing thing that this awful disease brought me a girl half my age, who, in less than fifteen minutes, taught me to love life for simply what it is*, she thought, smiling to herself.

3

Was There a Defining Moment in Your Life That Made You Who You Are Today?

I figured out that I could do anything I set my mind to.
—Summary answer from 100 women's surveys

There are moments in life that force us to choose between surviving and succumbing. I call these defining moments. What makes us delve further than ever into our souls and grow stronger than we ever thought possible? This is when you come face-to-face with your core and the depth of your personal human spirit. This is when you say to yourself, *If I can handle this, I can handle anything*!

As I read the survey responses, I was heartbroken that there were so many replies that involved domestic violence. It takes tremendous courage to leave an unhealthy situation, especially when children are involved. According to recent statistics, one in four women in the United States will experience violence at the hands of an intimate partner during their lifetime.

Let that statistic sink in ... 25 percent of us will know what it feels like to be physically abused by someone we trusted most. How can we, as a group, allow that to go on? Simply put, we cannot. Thinking the victim needs to do something before you take action is faulty reasoning. The victim is often the one person least capable of saving herself. Putting an end to domestic violence is everyone's business, so if you suspect it, do something. If you are currently in a relationship that does not make you feel physically or emotionally safe, get out. Period.

> *I will never forget the way you made me feel—*
> *like I was everything. And I will never forget the*
> *way you made me feel—like I was nothing.*
> —Antonio M. Arce

Tanya's Story

The door to the garage slammed shut. He was inside the house. In the shadows, Tanya quickly turned onto her side so she could see Mick's silhouette when he came through the bedroom door. She consciously slowed her breathing, hoping he would think she was asleep so he wouldn't accuse her of waiting for him so she could start a fight. She willed every cell of her body to listen intently, sensing for cues of what was about to come.

How had it come to this? So many nights she would wait in the darkness to see what person would stop by the bed and stare down at her. It may have been the same body each time, but it was definitely not the same man. Some nights, when he hadn't been drinking, the Mick she'd known four years ago would wrap himself around her and hold her with a tenderness and care she'd never experienced anywhere else. Other nights, most nights, the Mick who had emerged since Dana had been born three years ago would arrive with an angry agenda, sometimes punctuated with a fist.

Tanya had been 22, fresh out of college and optimistic about all that life had to offer. She'd completed her undergraduate degree with a spellbinding violin solo during the senior concert. She knew how to put her soul forth when performing, how to give her whole heart to a piece of music. Mick had emerged from the audience and approached her after that concert, telling her what an incredible talent she was. He'd attended it to hear his younger brother, Roger, play the clarinet, and afterward he joined the group of graduating seniors who had gone out for pizza and beer to celebrate. He kept a polite distance that evening, but Tanya had known he'd watched her all evening, and she'd done all she could to keep his attention. After a while she noticed that he'd left the party before they had a chance to talk to each other again. She slept alone that night with Mick on her mind.

Later that week Mick had become another page in Tanya's mental scrapbook of college experiences. When she'd returned to her parent's house in an upper-middle class suburb of Chicago, her father had begun asking her what was next. Graduate school was out of the question for fall because she'd missed all the application deadlines— something that irritated her father to no end. She spent most mornings combing through job websites, but a bachelor's degree in music didn't seem to be getting her anywhere near self-supportive. At the precise moment Tanya was resentfully conceding to the reality of having to return to the steakhouse she'd worked in as a waitress during her summers, the doorbell rang.

A teenage boy in a white Polo shirt stood on the front porch with a large red rose embroidered on it. In his arms was a two-foot long white box tied with a gigantic blue ribbon. There was a van in the driveway that read "Bella Flowers" on the side in ridiculously ornate scroll.

"I'm looking foooor, uhhhh, Tanya Weber?" asked the boy as he read the delivery instructions. At that very moment Tanya's mother came up behind her and reached forward with a five-dollar bill.

"This *is* Tanya Weber! Thank you!" her mother said as she exchanged the tip for the box. The boy gladly handed the flowers over, stuffed the money in his right pants pocket, and was in the van before Tanya could even say thank you. Her mother had already dashed to the kitchen, opened the box, and was preparing a vase when Tanya entered, still perplexed by this surprise gift.

"And who, pray tell, are these from?" her mother sang. "You never mentioned anyone, but obviously some young man is putting his heart out to you."

"Honestly, I don't know," said Tanya, to which her mother rolled her eyes in exasperation. "Where's the card?"

"Right there! Open it!" her mother pointed to the small linen envelope on the kitchen counter. Tanya reached for it, hesitating because she recognized that this was the first time anyone had ever sent her flowers, and there would never be another first time again. She was old enough to understand this would be a cherished moment in her life that she would reminiscence about in her eighties and young enough to be thoroughly love-struck with whoever had sent the twelve long-stemmed, deep red, *perfect-in-every-way* roses. She fingered the envelope for a moment, appreciating its fine texture.

"For God's sake! Open it, Tanya! I'm dying here!" wailed her mother.

Tanya pulled the card three-quarters of the way out of the envelope and held it between her thumb and forefinger.

I can't stop thinking about you.
Vulnerably yours, Mick.

Their September wedding was spectacular.

Tanya's family had fallen in love with Mick almost as deeply as Tanya and Mick had fallen in love with one another. Tanya's father had offered Mick a position in his law firm located in a downtown Chicago high-rise, but Mick's family was entrenched in real estate development in Seattle and already had him earning a six-figure salary. Their Hawaiian honeymoon was followed by a 6,000 square-foot home purchase in the chic Queen Anne neighborhood. Mick surprised Tanya with a room redesigned with perfect acoustics for her music and a Stradivarius violin from the 18th century. Next came the BMW and an American Express card that allowed Tanya to explore Seattle and buy whatever caught her eye. Mick dug into his work with Tanya's full support.

Their weekends were filled with dinners and drinks with Mick's family's business associates. Tanya spent her days seeking out new recipes to try in both the kitchen and the bedroom. From Tanya's point of view, life was perfect. She wanted for nothing, she had no pressures, and she was *head over heels* in love. She just wished she could get that nagging sense of disquiet out of her gut. There was no discernable reason for it; she had a life that most women could only dream of.

Mick asked Tanya to stop her birth control pills on their wedding night. He let her know that he and his family wanted them to have children sooner rather than later, and within the first six months of their marriage, Tanya gave him the happy news that they would be parents just after their second Christmas. Mick drove her to every doctor's appointment and was by her side at every Lamaze class. He doted on Tanya during her pregnancy, calling her several times a day to check in, and even accompanied her to the grocery store and gym.

Although Tanya had resisted, Mick insisted on finding out if it was a boy or a girl as soon as they could. It was a girl, which produced a flurry of shopping for pink things. Mick asked if they could name their daughter after his mother, Dana. Tanya had always liked the name Ashley but acquiesced to Mick's plea. She had figured that any man who admired his mother that much would treat his wife with the same respect as the years went by.

Sounds of Mick rummaging around in the kitchen brought Tanya back to the present. Tanya had prepared him a plate of food and left it in the refrigerator, just as Mick had insisted was her duty. She heard him put it in the microwave and swear at something. Then she heard the glass from a bottle of whisky clink against the counter. Tanya let her breath out. He had poured himself another drink. That meant he wouldn't be in the bedroom for at least 10 minutes. Good. She was safe for at least another 10 minutes.

The first sign that something was awry showed up the day they brought Dana home from the hospital. Mick had forgotten to bring the baby car seat. When the discharge nurse told him that the hospital could not let him leave with the baby until he had a car seat, Tanya saw anger in Mick that was explosive. He had stood in the hospital's foyer and simply lost it, yelling obscenities and making threats until security escorted him out the doors. An hour later, Mick's brother, Roger, arrived to pick up Tanya and Dana. Roger was apologetic about Mick not being able to get them, but obviously had no idea how bad the scene was since he criticized the hospital staff for being so uptight. When they arrived at their house, Mick was drinking scotch in the living room. No apology or explanation was offered, and within a few minutes Mick left with his brother to go back to the office. They never spoke of the incident again, but it was the smoke of a fire that would soon burn their lives to the ground.

Over the next year, scotch became Mick's preferred companion. His tender attentions went to Dana, which both comforted and confused Tanya. On the one hand, she loved Mick deeply and completely. Seeing how gentle he was with Dana melted her heart. But on the other hand, her devotion to her husband was never enough to bring Mick out of his dark moods, which were lasting longer and longer. Things grew cooler between of them.

When Dana's first birthday arrived, Mick marked the occasion by selling Tanya's car. He told her that he constantly worried about her driving in the busy city traffic with their baby. He said he'd take her wherever she needed to go; that way she could sit in the backseat with Dana.

Since she moved to Seattle, Tanya had not had opportunities to create trusting friendships with the other women in Mick's family, and she had made only a few acquaintances outside of their family circle. Roger's wife, Carrie, was close to Tanya's age and also had a toddler, so she seemed like an obvious choice for friendship. Since Tanya had plenty of time to think about things now that she didn't go out during the day, she began planning the extended family Thanksgiving dinner at their house. Mick loved the idea of usurping the host position of one of his family's holiday dinners, which were usually held at his parents' home. It was still four months away, but Tanya was compelled to blueprint every nanosecond and detail of the event so she could get Carrie alone for at least a few minutes. It did not escape Tanya that she had begun plotting rather than planning. Fear and isolation motivate strangely unexpected behavior.

Thanksgiving came, and Tanya's preparations for the feast came together flawlessly. She'd hired caterers and servers, decorated the house, and even prepared a slideshow of Mick's family's photos for everyone to watch after the meal. While the hired help cleaned up and the men settled into the living room with cigars and scotch, Tanya went in search of Carrie. She found her in Dana's bedroom playing with Dana and her own toddler son. It could not have been more perfect for what Tanya wanted to do. She sat down on the floor next to Carrie so they could both watch their children, warmed things up with the usual chit-chat of how hard it is to be a mother, and then launched into the script she'd been reworking for months.

"So, how's married life since the little guy came along?" asked Tanya.

"Well, it's changed a lot of things—all the stuff you read in the books. Sleep, time alone, sex—it all goes out the window," replied Carrie. "Plus, Roger's been so tied up with the Ballard project, he's almost never home."

"Ballard project? Does Roger talk to you about his business? Mick never says a word." The conversation was taking an unexpected turn, but Tanya knew she needed to follow it.

"You're kidding, right? Mick didn't tell you the trouble they're having? They've started divesting all over the place, they're in a half-dozen lawsuits, and everyone had to take a pay cut to keep things going." The truth tumbled out of Carrie's loose lips. When she realized what she'd let drop, she sat up straight and grabbed Tanya's arm. "Oh my God, don't tell Mick I just told you all that. He needs to tell you himself. Promise me you won't tell him I told you!"

"Of course not, Carrie. Don't worry; we wives need to stick together, right?" Tanya felt pieces of the puzzle that had bewildered her the past year falling into place. Her heart softened at the notion that Mick had tried to shield her from his financial worries. Tomorrow, on that wonderfully quiet day after Thanksgiving, she'd have a conversation with Mick that would make everything right. All she needed to do was let him know she was beside him all the way, ready to weather any storm, and that she was proud of him no matter what.

Tanya heard Mick's footsteps on the stairs. He stumbled, then tripped and swore. He was drunk. Tanya's heart quickened until she could hear it in her ears. This was not going to be good. He was on the landing, plodding down the hall. He stopped at Dana's door and paused, then opened it a crack to peer in. Tanya heard the door close again, and a flood of conflicting feelings rushed through her. How could a man who consistently moved her with his love for his child also cause her to fear him so much? She deeply loved Dana's father. She was totally terrified of her husband.

The next day Dana played quietly at Mick's feet while he watched football. Tanya was feeling better than she had in two years, knowing that by the end of today her marriage would be stronger, Mick's anger would dissolve because he'd finally have someone he could share the load with, and he would acknowledge Tanya as his best friend and soul mate. She waited for halftime, took a plate of snacks into the living room, and curled up on the couch, facing Mick.

"Hey, babe, can we talk a minute?" cooed Tanya.

"Talk. Ah, shit. What's the matter now? This isn't going to take longer than halftime, is it? The Seahawks are winning." This was not exactly the answer Tanya had been hoping for, but she kept moving forward since she knew how sweet the ending would be for them both.

"I just want to tell you that I know about the trouble you're having at work and all the pressure you're under ..." Tanya saw Mick's eyes flash, saw his hand come up, and then saw nothing else until she woke up on the floor next to Dana, who was crying hysterically. Mick stood over her pointing his finger only a few inches over her face. It took a few seconds for Tanya to begin to comprehend what he was saying.

"You mind *your* business, and you leave me to mine. And *your* business is keeping this house clean and that kid quiet! You're so stupid! Do you actually think you could tell me anything I don't already know? Don't you *ever*, and I mean *ever*, talk to me, or anyone in my family, about business again. Do you hear me? If I *ever* find out you've been spying on me again, I'll have to do *this* again!"

Mick swung his fist in front of her nose, barely missing her face. Tanya instinctively closed her eyes and covered her face. Mick grabbed her wrist and yanked her to her feet. "Don't you give me that battered wife bullshit! Put your hands down! You deserved that slap, and you know it! You begged for it! You know how it pisses me off when you go sneaking around behind my back. *Look at me when I'm talking to you, bitch!*"

Tanya's thoughts were spinning. Her mind said she needed to put her hands down and look at him in order to end this, but her body was intent on protecting her face. She mustered every shred of courage she could find to look at him, but stepped back just far enough to be out of his arm's reach.

"There, happy now?" Mick spewed venomously as he turned and sauntered to the liquor cabinet. "Once again, you've ruined another fine family day together. Take Dana and get out of my sight. You make me sick."

Tanya picked up Dana and made a beeline for the bedroom. She held and rocked her daughter until she was asleep in her arms. She hugged her tight, feeling as though the love for her child was the only thing in her life that had not been utterly destroyed in the past 15 minutes. Finally, tears came. Tanya sobbed silently, afraid that Mick might hear her and come to punish her for it. Two hours later, Tanya heard the front door close and Mick drive away.

That was two and a half years ago. In 18 months Tanya and Mick had grown into a pattern of controller and controlled. When the day came that Mick came home and announced that he'd sold the house and Tanya needed to learn how to live on less, she didn't ask one question or show remorse of any kind. He hit her anyway, saying if she hadn't spent so much money all the time they wouldn't be in this position. When Mick discovered Tanya had invited Carrie over for coffee and a play date without asking him, he tried to push her down the stairs. When she didn't fall, he slapped her around until she lost control of her bladder. When Tanya did an Internet search for battered women's shelters, she received an immediate phone call from Mick shouting at her that he'd installed a monitoring program on her computer and just what the hell was she doing looking at abuse websites. The bruises and cuts had just enough time to heal between beatings, so Mick took over the grocery shopping so Tanya wouldn't been seen in public. He sat in on her hair, nail, and doctor's appointments to make sure "hen clucking," as he called it, didn't cross his personal line of marital confidentiality. He cancelled her credit cards. He had her name taken off the bank accounts. He had all their mail directed to his office and read her mother's letters to her before bringing them home. Almost 1,000 days of Tanya's life had been spent in fear, imprisoned in her own home, having her every moment and intention questioned.

And now, just 10 days short of their fourth wedding anniversary, at two o'clock in the morning, Tanya lay in her darkened bedroom quaking at Mick's advancing footsteps in the hall. She smelled him when he entered the room and crossed to their bed. He'd stopped, and she could feel him staring at her. She could feel his rage, his disgust with everything about her, his loathing that she was even alive. She didn't move, didn't breathe. She heard the fabric of his shirt move, and sensed his arm was raised. Squinting through her eyelashes, she saw a sliver of light glint off metal. He had a golf club raised over his head. Tanya's hands flew to cover her face and her body tucked in the fetal position, preparing for the blow to come.

Then came the loud thud. Tanya's body laid coiled for several seconds with her eyes squeezed shut. Finally, she gasped for breath after having held it for so long. She blinked, but saw Mick nowhere in the room. Apprehensively, Tanya sat up and reached for the light, her heart pounding in her ears. The tiny bedside lamp seemed like a stadium floodlight when it flicked on, and it took a moment for her eyes to adjust. But when they did, the first thing she saw was Mick lying in a heap beside the bed, the golf club still in his hand. She stared at him long enough to believe he would not zap back to consciousness at her tiniest movement. He was snoring, and drool was stringing out the side of his mouth. Tanya gathered her courage and shook his shoulder. Nothing. A state of euphoria filled her every cell.

Tanya took Mick's cell phone out of his pocket and calmly dialed 911. She smiled as she pictured herself dumping the Ambien Carrie had given her during their lunch into the whiskey bottle that afternoon. She had done it, and it had worked. Mick wasn't dead (but would soon wish he was), and neither was she. That was the best her life had been for a very long time.

"Nine-one-one. What is your emergency?"

Tanya had to think about that question for just a second before she answered.

"My husband beats me. I need someone to come get my daughter and me out of here. And, oh, you'd better bring an ambulance and handcuffs for my husbastard."

4

What Are You Most Proud Of?

I have learned and grown from the challenges
life has sent me rather than giving in to the
defeat they may first appear to be.
—Summary answer from 100 women's surveys

Becoming our best selves is never a magic wand transformation; it's a home built brick by brick that is torn down often and more thoughtfully recreated. We often forget to step back and appreciate the tremendous lives we create and the enormous obstacles we overcome. Taking a moment to be proud that we have stayed the course and triumphed is well deserved and honors all those who helped us along the way.

Nearly every survey respondent wrote of having a broken heart at some point in her life. The tales of rough divorces were particularly penetrating, especially when children were involved. It is one of the paradoxes of life that our greatest loves are the only people who have the power to hurt us so intensely. However, without exception, the pain brought self-knowledge and wisdom that made moving on and personal growth possible.

I'm proud of my heart. It's been played, stabbed, cheated, burned and broken. Yet, somehow it still works.
—Unknown

Grace's Story

Grace picked at her hangnail until it stung and a droplet of red appeared. It was a nasty habit that she'd had as far back as she could remember. Whenever she started picking over something mentally, she started picking at her cuticles. She slipped her finger in her mouth to soothe the sting and dove deeper into her mental conversation with herself.

She was sitting on the floor in the small space between the bed and the mirrored closet doors. Staring straight ahead into her reflection, she did not see herself. The noise in her head drowned out the perceptions from all her other senses. How could he have done this to her? To their family? The man she had believed she knew *everything* about had become a stranger in the few seconds it took her to read the text message on his phone. Now she couldn't be sure of *anything* about him. If Kevin could be sleeping with his assistant, it now felt as though there was nothing that Kevin would not do. Grace had been so sure of their marriage. The evening hours spent at his office never gave her so much as a twinge of suspicion. She even bragged to her family and friends about what a hard worker he was, so devoted to his family that he'd go the extra mile to make sure they wanted for nothing. This could not be happening. There had to be a logical explanation.

She picked up Kevin's phone and reread the message. "I miss you so much. I can't wait until you caress me in your arms again." Grace felt a searing hot pain rush from her heart and radiate through her entire body. She had never felt anything like it before and could not yet name it as humiliation or jealousy or betrayal. She only knew it hurt more intensely than anything she'd ever suffered.

At that moment, she heard Kevin's car pull in the driveway and hurried steps through the front door. When he entered the bedroom and found Grace sitting on the floor reading his texts, the words that were the final arrow through Grace's heart rushed out of his mouth before his brain could engage. "Oh, shit!"

One week later, Grace and her two toddlers, Matt and Cindy, four and two respectively, moved in with her parents. She was across the state from Kevin, but still far too close to the memories and emotions that went with them. As events unfolded and Grace's world crashed down around her ears, she learned from several of their friends that Kevin had never been faithful to her, their marriage, or their family. Grace found out that family and friends had known about Kevin's many affairs for years but had wanted to protect her from it by keeping silent. Now one after another came forward until Grace was so emotionally pummeled she was numb to it.

Grace's parents paid for a preschool for the children so she would have a few blessed hours a day to see a therapist, reflect, cry, and heal. Kevin took the lead in filing for divorce and was fair, even generous, with sending money until child support and alimony could be established. Even though he had made no attempt to keep Grace from leaving and spewed blame on her every chance he got, it was clear that he loved his children and did not want them to pay for their parents' mistakes. Grace wondered if that would change as the years went by. Her father's lawyer was thankfully representing her, and she felt confident that she could trust him to negotiate the best settlement possible. She agreed to let Kevin talk to the kids on the phone once a week, until Grace learned that his assistant, now living in the debilitating insecurity of a relationship with a cheater, demanded that she be in the room each time he called. Grace was unable to bear the mental image of the other woman in her house, rearranging her furniture, sleeping in her bed, and told Kevin so. Much to Kevin's sorrow, they agreed to no communication until the divorce was final. Matt and Cindy had long been accustomed to Kevin not being very present in their lives and adjusted to their new routines quickly. Grace envied their resilience.

Six months passed. The divorce, while painful, had been quick. Alimony and child support were helpful, but not enough to make it possible for Grace to move out of her parent's home and into a place of her own. While she was grateful beyond words for her mother and father's support, she felt that she could not begin putting her life back together until she and her children achieved independence. Her mother helped her pump up her resume and took her shopping for a business suit to wear to interviews. But after weeks of combing employment websites, attending job fairs and networking functions, and completing dozens of applications and not receiving so much as a nibble from prospective employers, Grace resigned herself to the fact that she may not be capable of supporting herself and her children.

Late one evening, Grace sat in the dark in her parent's living room, waiting for her glass of wine and bowl of ice cream to take the edge off her anxiety. She reprimanded herself for how utterly dependent she had been on Kevin and for not making more of herself. At the end of the day she'd been a spoiled, kept woman who wasted her hours on social media, mommy blogs, and shopping websites. While the support and sense of connection she experienced during the past months through Facebook and Twitter had saved her sanity, even her parents had expressed concern about how much time she spent on the Internet. She fell asleep on the couch, full of self-loathing and hopelessness. A few hours into the night, she crawled into bed next to her sleeping children and cried herself back to sleep.

The next morning, Grace awoke to find Matt and Cindy sitting in bed next to her, playing games on her laptop. She turned on a Disney movie to distract them so she could slip her computer away and check her Facebook page. It suddenly hit her—she had not mentioned the one thing she was an expert in on her resume: social media. Twitter, Instagram, Pinterest, and Facebook had been her delicate tether to the last remaining shreds of her self-esteem the past few months. Surely she could not be the only person who clung to these platforms like the life rafts from a sinking ship. Even more, her aptitudes on these had to be valuable to some employer. She went to her favorite employment website and for the first time typed in "social media." Page after page scrolled onto the screen with dozens of creative job titles such as Growth Hacker and Social Media Evangelist. Most of them mentioned marketing and asked for work experience, but for the first time in weeks Grace felt self-confident that her personal expertise was enough to nail these jobs. Her spirits soared, and she knew she was on the right track.

The next time Grace looked at the clock it was well past noon. Her mother had thankfully taken Matt and Cindy to daycare. By the time they returned, Grace had responded to 27 job listings from wildly varied businesses that all asked for social media experience. Grace had never been religious, but when she went to bed that night she literally got on her knees and asked the angels for help.

The dawn sunlight peeped from the narrow opening between the curtains. Grace had been awake for hours, her mind bouncing from one job advertisement to another, going from her inner voice telling her that she would never amount to anything to the gnawing fear that never seemed to leave her gut. Her laptop was on the nightstand beside her; she stared at it for a long time, mustering the courage to see if anyone had responded to one of her applications. Sitting up, she took a deep breath and opened the lid. Her e-mail inbox read zero new messages, and her heart plummeted. How could she have been so naïve to think it would happen quickly, with only one day's effort? How could she think there was anything that made her stand out from the hundreds of other people who had applied for those jobs? There were whole college degrees in social media now; she'd never be able to compete against that credential. She squeezed her eyes shut and let the tears flow.

But then she heard the familiar ping of an incoming e-mail. She grabbed her laptop, sure it was the early morning onslaught of junk mail. But maybe, *just maybe* …

Her inbox showed one new message, and Grace's stomach did a summersault when she saw it was a reply to an e-mail she'd sent.

"Dear Ms. Franklin." Grace noted that she needed to have her last name changed to back to Goodwin as soon as possible, and she would never change it again.

> *Thank you very much for applying for the position of Communication Specialist within our marketing department. We would like to arrange an interview with you at your earliest convenience. Please call the number below to set up a time.*
>
> *Warmest Regards,*
> *Beth Hogan, VP of Marketing*
> *Write On Media*

Grace squealed with glee. She reread the message five times, letting the title Communication Specialist sink in and gird her self-image. It was just past seven in the morning, and no one else in the house was moving yet. Grace tiptoed out to the kitchen where her voice wouldn't wake anyone up and dialed the number at the bottom of the e-mail.

At noon, Grace was sitting in the Beth Hogan's office forcing every cell in her body to focus, listen, and respond intelligently. Beth was an attractive woman in her mid-fifties with dark hair pulled into a loose bun. A streak of gray from her temple gave her an undeniable air of elegance and assurance. Her black suit was expertly fitted to compliment her slim figure. Grace recognized Beth's shoes as Jimmy Choo and her bracelet as Paloma Picasso. After half an hour of questions that tested Grace's knowledge of different social media platforms, not only did she come to like Beth, she wanted to *be* Beth.

"It's obvious that you know Facebook and Twitter really well," smiled Beth. "You could be a big help to our marketing team. But what's going on that you appear to have no recent job history or professional references?" Grace stopped breathing and stared into Beth's eyes. She didn't know if it was appropriate to spill your guts during a job interview or make up some polite way of sidestepping the question.

At that very moment, Grace's angels answered her prayer. She very clearly heard them whisper in her ear, *"Don't you dare lie to this women. She'll know it, and you'll blow it. Just give it to her straight."*

"I'm recently divorced. I've spent the past decade taking care of my ex-husband and two children. Now I need to make a life of my own and support my kids by myself. I know you'd be taking a chance by hiring me, but I promise you that someday you'll consider it the best decision you ever made." Beth's right eyebrow lifted slightly, and she looked Grace in the eye for what seemed like forever. Grace could feel her heart pounding. The silence in the room was palpable, but she would not drop Beth's gaze. Finally, Beth spoke.

"I'll hold you to that promise. Be here Monday morning at eight o'clock."

Seven years later, Grace sat behind Beth's desk. She had learned the hard business lessons of choosing to be effective over being right, that she was entitled to nothing, and that persistence and determination were more valuable than talent.

Beth gave Grace the chance to prove herself and eventually became her openly acknowledged mentor. Having been a mom herself, she understood when Grace had to leave work to take care of her kids, but she never moved a deadline to accommodate it. Grace had to figure out on her own how to meet her obligations, get tough, and keep up—although her Facebook friends were always there to help and support her.

By the time alimony and child support ran out, Grace was earning more than Kevin ever had during their marriage. Boyfriends came and went, but no one could divert Grace from her work or children. She had learned to take care of herself inside and out. She was all she ever needed.

5

Who Influenced You the Most?

The most trustworthy guide in my life
has been my own inner voice.
—Summary answer from 100 women's surveys

I found in these answers that it only takes one person to change everything in another's life. I think it is important for us each to be mindful that we may be that person for someone else. Sometimes all it takes is letting another person know that we see her greatness, even if she cannot. That was the consistent point in all these answers: that someone helped us understand ourselves better.

I know for myself, my parents were a huge influence in my life. My dad taught me to keep exploring and keep an open mind. My mom taught me to be true to myself and trust my inner voice. When I look back on who I have become, I can clearly see a beautiful blending of them both, along with the hundreds of other people who have been kind enough to invest themselves in me. That is what I want to be for others: a positive influence who consistently reminds people of their own magnificence and power.

> *I am sure that if the mothers of*
> *various nations could meet,*
> *there would be no more wars.*
> —E. M. Forster

Andrea's Story

Just before last Christmas, a friend asked Andrea to participate in a survey she was conducting for her motivational speaking business. Andrea agreed because she pictured the kind of survey you get from any company that has a customer service hotline. You know—the ones that have four or five questions about how satisfied you were, and you answer with either a 10 because you're feeling magnanimous toward the person in India who spoke to you, or a one because the person you talked to did not issue you the refund you were hoping for. Instead, Andrea's friend e-mailed her a page with questions that, much to her dismay, required essay answers and deep reflection, two of her least favorite things. Andrea let that e-mail sit in her inbox for six weeks, looking at it every day and wondering if it wouldn't just be easier to move to a different state and lose touch with that friend. Finally, the dreaded happened, and she ran into her friend in the grocery store.

"Heeeeeyyyyy! How are yooooouuuu?" Andrea sang out, trying to not let her face reveal that Andrea knew that her friend knew that she had broken her word about that damn survey. Her friend was kind and didn't bring the subject up. But when Andrea looked at it still sitting in her inbox, she thought she had better just get it done so she wasn't looking over her shoulder everywhere she went. So with a double-click, she dug in to get it over with as fast as she could.

1. What is your age? *48*
2. What is your profession? *Realtor*
3. Are you married? *Yes.* If yes, is this your first marriage? *Yes.*
4. Do you have children? *Yes.* If yes, what are their ages? *10, 13, 15.*
5. Please describe your relationship with your mother. *It's better than it's ever been. She's dead.*

Andrea stopped and stared at the lifetime of cynicism captured by her answer to the fifth question. Did she really want her friend to know that about her? Did Andrea want *anyone* to know that about her? What did it say about her that she still resented her mother for being, well, a cold-hearted psycho?

Andrea's mother, Marjorie Ruth Brown, was born in 1922 and died, exactly as she had always predicted, when she was 80 years old. Andrea thought that probably in the 1920s, 80 years seemed like a lot, but as it became common toward the end of the millennium, her mother's obstinate nature refused to be proven wrong. By the time she was

78, Elvis had left the building of her brain, taking every coherent shred of her mind with him. The Alzheimer's Care Center staff found her dead in her bed three months to the day after her 80th birthday. Andrea's first child, Jason, had been born just four months prior. Marjorie had never met him. In the scores of photographs Andrea sent her, Marjorie never even comprehended that Jason was her first grandchild. She never found peace in knowing that, if her life had meant nothing else, her existence had made it possible for Andrea's three beautiful, kind children to be brought into the world.

Marjorie had been the first person in her extended family to ever graduate from college. Andrea had proudly hung her diploma from Oklahoma State University in her office and looked at it often. Her mother had graduated with a major in psychology in a day when women had been generally relegated to teaching or nursing. However, World War I was placing more and more women in the workplace, and universities were hurting for enrollment. Marjorie's timing could not have been better. She studied Freud and Jung during the height of their groundbreaking theories. She worked as a telephone operator five shifts a week, lived in the spare bedroom of family friends in exchange for childcare, and had the one photograph taken of her that she ever liked. As a teenager, Andrea used to look intently into the face in that picture for long periods of time, trying to make sense of what seemed impossible: that her mother had once been her age.

Soon after Marjorie's college graduation, Andrea's parents met one another. After her father's military service as a Morse code operator on an aircraft carrier, he had come back to his home state of Texas and taken advantage of the GI Bill. He had lost his brother during the war and felt obligated to make his parents proud of their only living child by also being the first in his family to get a college degree. He wanted to be a writer, so he majored in journalism.

He had landed a job with a paper in Anchorage and was sent a ticket to fly out of the airport closest to him, Oklahoma City. He had decided to take some friends with him for a weekend of youthful farewell partying, and they met Andrea's mother and her group of friends coming out of a theatre showing of the movie *Mildred Pierce*. Andrea watched that film a dozen times and always found it interesting that it was one of the first self-made-woman stories to gain popularity. No doubt, her mother saw her own spirit in Mildred. One thing led to another, and Marjorie soon found herself on a plane headed for Alaska and her wedding.

Nothing about that phase of Andrea's mother's life ever added up. The woman whom Andrea knew as her mother was angry and headstrong and paranoid. Who was that young, fresh face in the photo who wanted to know what made people tick? Who worked and studied 24/7 and lived on determination alone while she went to college? Who set off for the unknown, wild lands of Alaska in the late 1940s to have a wedding with not one person she knew in attendance? What had happened that made her lose her courage, her fire, and her dreams? Why, when most people mellow and gain wisdom as they grow old, had she become even more self-centered? Why was she livid with the life she said her husband had forced her into? And most of all, why was she distant from her children?

After two years of freezing and having no social life whatsoever, Andrea's father was transferred to Los Angeles to work at the *LA Times*. Her mother had not been able to work at all in Alaska, and she set her sights on getting a job with the VA's booming psychiatric division. However, just before they left Anchorage, Marjorie found out she was pregnant. She was relieved to know that she'd be in civilization for the pregnancy and delivery but frustrated that her own career was put on hold again. *Mildred Pierce* had had a similar problem and ended up getting dumped by her husband and left penniless. Marjorie worried about that often.

The pregnancy was normal, and when labor started, Marjorie felt lucky to live in a modern time when mothers were anesthetized during childbirth to spare them from all the pain and gore. Fathers were relegated to the waiting room until all the private female-doings were over. Andrea's mother woke up to a sobbing husband who told her that their first child had died before it ever took a breath. Her father went back to work the next day, but Marjorie had to stay in the hospital the rest of the week, watching mothers in her shared room hold and nurse and love their newborn infants. Andrea tried to remember the pet name they had come up with for that baby, but couldn't. Now, as a mother, she understood how that gash on her mother's soul had never healed.

In an effort to cheer her up, Andrea's dad bought Marjorie the latest Singer sewing machine. Until the day she died, she told the story of how infuriated that made her. During dinner parties, Thanksgiving, or any other social event, she'd gather a group around her to hear her tale, ending it with a viper's hiss, "How could anyone be stupid enough to think a household appliance would compensate for the loss of a child?" People would nervously titter, uncomfortable with the very personal nature of the story, let alone her effort to humiliate her husband. He would just pour another glass of bourbon and tell a joke that made people laugh easily. He was the popular one, liked by everyone they knew. Their friends quickly labeled Marjorie *nuts*.

Over the next few years, Andrea's dad attended graduate school at night. Her mother convinced him that being a writer, especially in the newspaper business, was no way to support a family; being a professor was so much more respectable and consistent. By the middle of the 1960s they had four children—Andrea's older brother, two younger sisters, and her—and were living in the town where they would be raised.

Her dad was teaching journalism at the local state university, and her mom was trying to be June Clever. She wore a garter belt and stockings while she ran the Hoover around every room twice a day. The house and children were clean at five o'clock in the evening. Dinner was on the table by six with the four food groups unfailingly represented. Her father sipped bourbon and smoked cigarettes while he watched his hero, Walter

Cronkite. Andrea's mom supervised homework, baths, and bedtime. She was an expert administrator who was committed to the high standards she expected to be met in her home. For her, life was a giant checklist that needed to be completed on a daily basis, or she would be worthless.

When Andrea's youngest sister began grade school, Marjorie enrolled in graduate school in Education. Since her husband was an employee of the university, tuition was free. Andrea could still picture her so clearly, sitting at the dining room table surrounded by books and stacks of paper, cigarette in hand. When her mom had to take a statistics class, her dad faced down the danger of having another sewing machine-like story in his life and bought her the newest technological advancement: a Texas Instruments handheld calculator. Looking her husband straight in the eye, Marjorie said it would be cheating and that he'd only bought it for her because he didn't believe she was smart enough to do it on her own. When Andrea's sister packed up their mother's house after she moved into the Alzheimer's Care Center, she found that calculator, still in the box with a price tag of $295.00— almost a week's salary for a professor at the time. It never became a story held over his head, but it was the last significant gift Marjorie's husband ever bought her.

By the time Andrea was a freshman in high school, her mother was a professor of Education at the same university where her father worked. She constantly complained about the sexism, a word used only by bitchy women at the time. She was paid half what male professors of Education were making and was given no benefits whatsoever. The official explanation was that married couples didn't need two benefits packages because the husband's took care of them both. They worked until Andrea's father had a heart attack at age 64 and was forced into retirement. Marjorie left her position at the same time because "his retirement's not enough to hire someone to take care of him."

One by one, Marjorie's children fled the coup as soon as they could. Andrea's brother moved to a city 80 miles away the day after he graduated from high school. Two years later, Andrea moved into the dorms at the university and made sure to avoid journalism and education classes. Her younger sisters escaped to towns across the state as soon as they turned 18. The only time they were all in the same room together again was a few Christmas holidays and when their dad died. From time to time, one or two of them would go to each other's weddings. Phone calls for birthdays or graduations or births were never made. During the rare conversations, it soon became clear that the only thing they had in common with each other was their mutual resentment of their mother. Andrea and her youngest sister admitted to each other that they'd been in therapy for years, trying to work through the issues Marjorie had saddled them with. Andrea's brother married and had a child, but lost his job soon thereafter. He took over the homemaker role and never went back to work again. Andrea believed he grew to be the male version of their mother—angry and depressed.

While their father was alive, Andrea made every effort to go home at least once a year to check on him, knowing life alone with his wife would be tough. Marjorie had delineated an imaginary line down the middle of the house that staked out her and her husband's territories. In an effort to extract Andrea's dad's appreciation for all she had given up by being his wife, Marjorie stopped cooking his meals, doing his laundry, or cleaning his side of the house. "It's about time he learned how hard it's been all these years," summed it up for Marjorie. Whenever Andrea tried to talk to her about it, her mom would sigh and say, "Well, at least we've stayed together."

When Andrea's father died, all his children rushed home to support their mother. Surely this would be the one time in her life when she would need them. But after telling them there was no way she'd spend a dime on a burial or funeral for that son-of-a-bitch, she promised to send her husband's ashes to Andrea's brother and told them all to go home. The only one of her children who ever made an effort to see her again was her youngest, Jenny.

As Marjorie's health began to fail, Jenny took over her mother's finances, made sure medical care was arranged, and legal documents signed. Jenny did all this while she fought her own battle with breast cancer. Her siblings made themselves feel better by saying this only made sense, because Jenny lived the nearest to their mom and had no children to take care of. Aside from the fact that she had no hair, letting Jenny carry the load with Mom seemed just fine. When Jenny asked her mother to move in with her so it would be easier to care for her, Marjorie refused, saying, "With my luck, you'd die the day after I got there, and then what would Andrea do with me?"

While still deep in this reflection, Andrea's 13-year-old daughter, Kelly, came into the room. One look at Andrea's face and Kelly stopped in her tracks.

"Whoa. What's up with you? Did somebody die?" Kelly said, hoping to snap her mother out of it. It didn't work. Instead, tears filled Andrea's eyes, and she reached out her arms for Kelly.

"Mom, you're scaring me. What's wrong?" It dawned on Andrea that Kelly had never seen her lose it. Andrea was her mother's daughter when it came to always keeping herself together. That needed to change. Andrea wanted Kelly to know her, *really know her*.

"Everything's fine, baby. I just need a hug. I love you so much," Andrea said. Kelly allowed her mother to hold and rock her until Andrea let go and wiped her cheeks dry. "Sorry, I was just thinking about my mother. And I want to make sure you know how much I love you."

There was more to it than that, but Andrea didn't think Kelly could understand her realization that Andrea had been as hard on her mother as her mother had been on her. Granted, Marjorie was the adult at the time and Andrea the child, but more importantly, Marjorie raised her family during an era that didn't have open, honest conversations or encouraging circles of friends to support her the way Andrea's friends supported her. Marjorie had lived with unthinkable inequalities between the sexes and disrespect of women's intelligence. She was professionally sidelined into a "woman's" field and never paid enough to support herself. She had no friends around her when she lost her baby. She resented her husband for being handed the dreams that she had wanted for herself, but society had refused her. Her children didn't like her, and she had died alone.

5.   Please describe your relationship with your mother. ***It's better than it's ever been. She's dead.***

6.   Who influenced you the most in your life? ***My mother.***

Despite everything, her mother had taught Andrea what no one else could: the purpose of life is to be happy.

6

If You Could Live Your Life Again, What One Thing Would You Change?

I would be more kind, especially to myself.
—Summary answer from 100 women's surveys

It was heartening to read many women answer, "I wouldn't change a thing," to this question. But the other answers inspired me to look deeply at this for myself. Some wrote they would be less conforming, bolder in career and relationship choices. Many said they would have made more of their own choices instead of following those that other people made for them. The theme was consistently in line with wanting to live and not merely exist.

What was *between* the lines of these answers was awe-inspiring. Everyone wished they had been kinder, less hurried, less quick to judge, more loyal to people and causes in which they could have made a difference. The great news is if you're reading this, there's still time to make these changes!

He who trims himself to suit everyone
will soon whittle himself away.
—Raymond Hull

Monica & Haley's Story

2002

Monica smiled over at her daughter, Haley. They were having one of their mother-daughter days that included lunch, pedicures, and a short shopping expedition. Both of them were sitting in a pedicure chair, massage rollers on, feet in bubbly warm water, being expertly pampered by beautiful Asian girls. Haley had her attention riveted to a *New Yorker* magazine she had brought with her, obviously engrossed by some heady article. Monica thumbed through her *People* magazine and recalled the first time she'd seen Haley in exactly this same position; it had been on her sixth birthday, 12 years prior. Monica's gift to Haley had been a day with Mommy doing "big girl" things. They had both enjoyed it so much that it had become their tradition for both of their birthdays and every chance they got in between.

Haley looked up just in time to see her mother's smile and returned it with sincere affection. Her mother had always been the girly one between the two of them— prettier, more fun at parties, always paying attention to details like shoes and jewelry. Haley had always been more interested in books than boys, which she supposed was a good thing since she was short and on the plump side. Her mother had made every effort to reassure Haley that she was beautiful beyond words, but Haley's classmates had not been so kind. She learned to take the truth in stride and focus on something besides being popular.

Haley was now 18, just a month away from leaving for college. Over the years, she and her mother had been through much together: a divorce when Haley was four; a second marriage two years later; and the arrival of Haley's half-brother, Jason, when she was eight; and an affair with Monica's boss when Haley was 15 that had been the cause of a legal separation that lasted six months. Raising Jason together had been the reason the couple reconciled. Monica had often leaned on Haley for support when things were emotionally tumultuous, which all their therapists had discouraged. But Haley felt it was good to be the practical, strong one; it made her mature beyond her years. While most of her friends were apprehensive about leaving home for college, Haley felt fully prepared to deal with adult life.

Their thoughts were interrupted by one of the nail techs presenting a tray of bottles of polish. "You pick color?" in broken English brought smiles and looks between the mother and daughter. They had made a ritual of choosing each other's color; it was an affectionate exchange that demonstrated how well they knew one another. Haley held up "Paint the Town Red," while Monica waved "Pale Pinkalicious," and they both smiled again. Monica was bold and flamboyant, Haley was a deep thinker and quiet.

Lunch was on the deck at Francesco's, Monica's favorite restaurant. It overlooked a pond, and Haley was tossing the last pieces of her bread to eager ducks below. Knowing that this would probably be the last day like this they would spend together until Haley returned from college next spring, both women turned inward a bit. Neither of them wanted to cry in front of the other people in the restaurant. Monica broke the tension by suggesting it was time to go shopping.

Haley took the project of college entrance very seriously. Her mother was pregnant with Haley when she graduated from high school and worked in office assistant positions since then. Her stepfather only intruded into Haley's life when she asked him to. That only happened twice: once in the sixth grade when it was *bring-your-dad-to-school* day, and once when she accidentally ran over the neighbor's cat backing out of the driveway. Other than that, Haley had been content to believe that she and her mother were a team, and Jason and her stepfather were a team, and these two teams just happened to live in the same house.

Beginning with her sophomore year in high school, Haley met with her school's academic counselors, wrote to college admissions departments, studied and took entrance exams, and even paid application fees out of money she'd earned tutoring. By the time Christmas of her senior year rolled around, four respected universities had accepted Haley. She went with the one that offered her a full-ride scholarship, relieved to know she would not have to work during college as long as she maintained her GPA.

2008

Haley quickly scanned the audience as she crossed the stage when her name was called to accept her diploma. She was looking for her mother. But how could she miss her? Monica was standing on her chair, cheering wildly. Haley knew that her mother could have no perception of the amount of hard work that had been required in order to finish her law degree. She had been home only for Christmas the past four years, devoting herself to internships during all her other breaks. Her single-minded determination had been rewarded with a position clerking for a judge in DC Circuit Court, starting as soon as she could make it there after graduation.

On the other hand, Haley's single-minded determination had punished her with a complete lack of romance at just the age when romance was all most girls thought of. During her college years, Haley had twice gone to bed with young men who were as awkward, lonely, and as tipsy as she was. She had not enjoyed the encounters and was always relieved when she got back to the library and her books—her homeland where she felt accomplished and in control.

Monica kicked off her shoes, checked to make sure her cleavage was not showing too much, and climbed up on her chair to root for Haley. Jason and her husband were with her, but not nearly as excited. When Haley left the stage, Monica climbed down and strutted toward her daughter; her daughter the *lawyer*; her daughter the *Washington DC lawyer*. Monica was so proud that she thought she might knock Haley over with the strength of her hug when she finally got to her. This was the daughter who proved to the world that even a knocked-up teenager could give the world something incredibly wonderful. Monica heard her own mother's voice in her head: *A little slut like* you *will never amount to anything. You've ruined your life and will be lucky to stay pretty long enough to find a man who'll put a roof over your sorry head in exchange for what's between your legs.* She now mentally replied to her mother with a sense of defiance and triumph she'd never allowed herself before: *Ha! Take this, Mom!* I, not *you, raised a really, truly smart girl who is strong and knows right from wrong. So at the end of the day, I have accomplished far more than you ever dreamed of!*

2012

Monica listened to the house creak as the sun rose and began to heat the roof. She had been sitting in her living room all night, not wanting to go to bed alone. Her husband left over a month ago. Once Jason graduated from college, her husband declared that he was done. He gave their marriage all he could so that he could be an active part of his son's life, but now there was no reason to continue the charade. Their marriage was never capable of surviving on its own. Christmas would arrive in just another two weeks, and Jason would most likely spend the holiday with his father, so Monica would wait until then to break the news of yet another failure in her life to her over-the-top successful daughter. In the meantime, there was packing to do and a future to figure out.

Haley looked at the Washington Monument out her office window. She had become one of the most promising young legal minds on Capitol Hill and a partner in a prestigious firm that advised elected officials from all over the country. Since her arrival in Washington DC, the pace of political events had been blindingly fast—there was so much changing in American society, but the law was lagging behind.

Haley wanted the law to lead people toward moral progress and dedicated herself to gay rights issues. There was much she wanted to accomplish and many lives she wanted to benefit from her work. She would continue to fight for others' rights to legal protections, even if it was not something she, herself, had ever personally experienced.

Haley let her gaze fall to the toes of her very practical black pumps and tried to remember the last time she had a pedicure. She immediately texted her mother to say she really wanted lunch at Francesco's and a day at the salon when she came home for Christmas. She could see Monica's smile in her mind's eye.

2014

Haley invited her mother to come to Washington for Christmas. The past two years' holiday seasons spent in Monica's small condominium were just too intense because there was no place for privacy. Both of them had grown to value their time in solitude. Haley had a spacious brownstone across the street from the Library of Congress where they each could have their own bed and bathroom. This way, when Monica started pressing Haley for information about the men in her life, which there were none, Haley could retreat and close the door. Also, Monica could take charge of creating a Christmas with a tree and decorations while Haley worked, which suited them both just fine. They would have 10 days and 10 nights together—a longer period of time than they'd had since Haley left for college.

As Monica packed, she felt an exhilaration she hadn't experienced for so many years. She was going to get on a plane and fly across the country! She had never been to Washington DC; in fact, she'd never been anywhere that couldn't be driven to within a day. Haley had always been too busy with work, and Jason's vacations had always been guy trips with his father. But since September when Haley had invited her to come for Christmas, Monica had devoured travel shows and tourist guidebooks about all the incredible things to see and do in the nation's capital. For the first time that she could recall, Monica allowed herself to experience the tingling sense of boundless possibility that travel to new places provides. Plus, she was single, still attractive, and hungry for adventure. When the taxi arrived in the early morning hours to take her to the airport, Monica looked at the lightly falling snow and felt like she was in a movie. Maybe, just maybe, *her* time had finally come.

After dropping suitcases off at Haley's flat, the two went immediately to a salon for pedicures; first things first. Haley felt herself relax deeply. There was no denying that as different as she and her mother were, they were each other's center. All was well when they were together. Once again, Haley admired how pretty her mother was, and Monica marveled at how self-confident and capable Haley was.

Over dinner Monica began to list all of the things she wanted to see and do, and Haley realized that even though she'd lived in DC for almost five years, she hadn't taken the time to see any of the local sights. She decided to shock her staff and let them know that she wouldn't be back to work until after New Year's Day.

The next morning Haley woke up to the smell of coffee. Padding out to the kitchen, she found Monica looking out the front window at the people on the sidewalk below. Turning to Haley, she said, "Let's get this place Christmas-fied." The sound of adventure and conquest immediately ignited them both. Quick showers and they were out the door, headed toward Chinatown on foot. They stopped at a coffee shop for breakfast, and over coffee they awkwardly began a conversation that had been avoided at their lunch date 12 years earlier.

"Mom, I am so happy you're here. I feel like I've been busy for a decade, and I just need a break," began Haley.

"Oh, Haley! Thank you for asking me! I needed a break too," replied Monica. This time neither cared that tears were welling already. "Baby, I know I say how proud I am of you all the time, but I don't think you really understand just how deep it goes. You've grown up to be everything I wanted to be, but I could never seem to get myself together enough to even get started. I respect you more than any other woman I know."

"Come on, Mom," Haley leaned in. "Tell the truth. You wish I were prettier, or that I at least had a boyfriend. I know I sure wish for those things. You've always been so at ease with yourself, so confident that you look good and don't have to prove yourself. I'd give anything to have that."

Monica sat back in her chair, mouth agape. "What? I don't wish you were prettier. I've never thought that! I think you're perfect the way you are! I've always thought *you* wished I was smarter, more of a professional woman."

This time Haley was shocked. "What? I think you're very smart! You had some tough breaks, and your mom never supported you the way you have me. I've always admired that you just do what has to be done, and get on with it. But at the same time, you've mastered men. I just don't get personal relationships at all."

Their plates of food were getting cold in front of them during the long silence that passed. They were both thinking, trying to make sense of the lightning bolt that had hit them individually but simultaneously.

Finally, Haley leaned in. "Do you think it's possible that we've both spent the past, say 20 years, wishing we were each other?"

Monica did not miss a beat. "Of course I wish I were you! Look at you! You're everything that any woman would want to be! Boyfriends? I'll teach you about boyfriends. They're easy!"

Haley smiled. "I guess that means we're going clothes shopping this afternoon, right? Tell you what, Mom, you teach me about men, and I'll teach you about college. With online universities being so available these days, you could have your degree in no time."

"Me? Go to college?" Monica squeaked. "Do you really think I could do it? I've always wanted to study interior design. Do you think there's an online program like that?" Haley's beaming face confirmed that she believed in her mother more than anyone.

*   *   *   *   *   *   *   *   *   *

Years later, when they recalled this conversation, both Monica and Haley termed it their "coin moment." They were the other side of each other's coin; inseparable, opposite, yet complete only when together.

7

What Do You Want Your Legacy to Be?

I want to leave many people a little
better than I found them.
—Summary answer from 100 women's surveys.

Terry's Legacy

I know—you were expecting another story. But this is my book (so there), and I'm going to take this opportunity while it's right in front of me to fulfill one of my life's goals: having you take the next few minutes to read these words, and let them change your life. This is exactly what I want my legacy to be. I want you to remember me as someone who loved you deeply, admired you for who you are, and helped you realize your dreams of a wonderful life and peaceful world.

If I close my eyes and picture you in my mind, I am absolutely spellbound by the beauty I see. You are surrounded by women who know your heart and love you.

I want to talk to you about your *Self,* the one that begins with a capital S. Your real Self, your spiritual Self. This is your journey into self-awareness; coming to know who you really are beyond your social mask, beyond your ego. I am not talking about religion or faith or anything like that. Don't get me wrong; I have the utmost respect for all religions and all practices. But our spirituality is the common divine thread that runs through every person who has ever lived before, lives now, and will ever come after us. We are all a part of this higher consciousness, more alike than we are different.

French philosopher Pierre Teilhard de Chardin said, "We are not human beings having a spiritual experience. We are spiritual beings having a human experience." Think about that deeply for a moment. Notice that there is a part of your consciousness that observes you while you think. It is not judging your thoughts and actions nor even commenting on them, only observing. I call this observer your soul. You don't *have* a soul; you *are* a soul. This is not your mind. Your mind is that relentless internal dialog. Your Being, your soul, is way beyond that. We don't call ourselves human *thinkings.* We don't call ourselves human *doings.* We call ourselves human *Beings.* This is the real you; this is your *Being,* and it is ever-present, all-loving, and all-wise.

When you ask, "'What is my life's purpose?'" there is a universal answer: to spend more and more and more of your time here on earth in the experience of Being. When we are *in* the experience of joy, compassion, love, we are *Being.* When we have those *aha* moments, spiritual insights, and intuitions that provide solutions to our problems, we are *Being*. There is a spiritual answer or solution to every question or problem, and we can discover it only when we are in the space of Being. You can tell when you're in a state of Being because your experience will be one of unity. The purpose of life for every single one of us is to fulfill the highest expression of ourselves as Beings.

Now you might be thinking, *But, Terry, how do I just be? This is too hard. I'll never be able to do it.* The great news is there is absolutely nothing more you need to do; you already are *Being*. The very nature of a human is to exist in that state of grace. What you're really asking me how to do is how to get your mind to shut up long enough to give you a chance to experience life without that internal dialog blaring in your head. I call that dialog your ego. Your ego is where your mind lives, and you can tell it's not your Being because it does not produce joy, compassion, love, creativity, and solutions. Like a machine out of control, it produces conflict, invalidation, and addictions of all kinds; it even makes you believe that your Being might not be real. How crazy is that? The insistent stream of judgment and discontent in your head will actually try to convince you that *it* is more real than your *Being*.

Here's another thing about Being: it only lives in the present moment, while your ego lives only in the past or the future. That makes this very moment the most important one in your life, and the person who is in front of you *right now* the most worthy person of your attention, and the thing you are doing *right now* the most vital thing you could be doing. The instant those three things are not true, you are not in a state of Being. When you slip out of being focused on this moment *right now*, you've become a victim of your memories and a pawn of your hopes. In the state of Being, you use your memories, they don't use you; you create and progress your hopes, not let them take you out of the profound appreciation of this moment right now. Human's natural state is one of Being. To snap yourself back into the peace and joy that is always present when you're Being, all you need to do is notice it.

Think of it like this: the natural human is naked, unadorned, undisguised. We lose our natural state of peace and harmony when we become unnatural by covering our nakedness with clothes, masks, or jewelry. This becomes a double-bind, because once we have the clothes on, we think becoming naked again could be dangerous, vulnerable. The longer we wear clothes, the more anxious we become when we think about returning to our natural selves. Then our egos even tell us that we're better off with clothes because we *look* so darn good! But here's the magic: to return to the state of naturalness, all we must do is notice the clothes. Just like the children's story of the *Emperor's New Clothes*, if we only look with intent to see the truth, we realize that we've been naked all along. *Now* is the moment that never ends, so it is always available to you by simply turning your attention to it.

"But I'm too busy to take the time to do this." It is almost become a cliché for not having the life you want.

Yet the more we try to complete that never-ending list of tasks on our to-do list, the further we seem to be from the happiness, abundance, and inner peace we yearn for. That is because we neglect to create our to-be list first. The common but flawed belief is that if we *do* something, we will *be* something. If we make more money, we will be happy. If we find the right life partner, we will be more loving. If we lose weight, we will be more beautiful.

This widespread *Do-Have-Be* belief is not in alignment with the universal law of *Being* as the catalyst of creation. Sages of all faiths have confirmed that the Universe works in the sequence of Be-Do-Have. To begin wrapping your head around this truth, take a look at what you want. Wealth? Affection? Inner Peace? Ask yourself what you would be if you had these. Contented? Inspired? Joyful? Now you know your starting point. If you focus on being content, the Universe will pour abundance into your life. If you follow your heart to inspiration, people will naturally want to be near you. If you allow yourself to experience the joy that is always waiting to be expressed, your head and heart cannot help but align, and inner peace will be yours.

That sounds crazy, right? But I know from my own experience that it is true! Test it for yourself. Tell yourself that you are happy, smile at someone who looks like they could use a lift, and then ask yourself how you are feeling. I guarantee your happiness will have increased. Once you are happy, inspired, and at peace, you will find that all those chores on your to-do list will begin to be completed with grace-filled ease. Make your mind up about what you will *be*, and the universal law of *Be-Do-Have* will be set in motion, blessing you with stress-free *do*'s and abundant *have*'s.

I invite you to relax and *be* rather than straining to become. Enjoy to the hilt Being in the present moment, just as it comes. I promise that when you do, you will feel the confining shell that has kept you limited crack open. You will soon be free to stretch the most exquisite wings ever seen and fly anywhere you like under a loving sun.

When I asked the Universe for strength,
I was given difficult situations to face.

When I asked the Universe for happiness,
I was shown how to lift another's spirit.

When I asked the Universe for wealth,
I was shown how to comfort those in need.

When I asked the Universe for peace,
I was shown how to help others.
— T.S.

8

What Do You Want Other Women to Know?

Every woman is so much stronger than she realizes.
—Summary answer from 100 women's surveys

The heart and inspiration for this book comes from the next story. The character Rosa is based on a dear friend whom I originally met when I hired her to clean my house nearly 10 years ago. Every time I see her, she has a smile on her face and love in her heart. We feel her essence when she is in our home.

At an unexpected point in our relationship, Rosa faced the unimaginable as a parent; the tragic loss of her son. Through her ordeal I personally witnessed grace, strength, and courage like I had never seen in my life. To this day I carry with me the lessons in fortitude that I learned from her. I now know that I can handle just about anything after seeing her deal with the loss of her son.

After that, I was curious in general about what made women stand up to heartache and peril when in reality they'd rather be doing anything else. I set out to find 100 women and ask them questions on the subject, and that's how *One Hundred Hearts* was born. Thank you, my friend, for sharing your intimate story so that other women can be inspired to do the same when faced with their own grave situations.

Rosa's Story

Ah, mi madre. Eres tan hermosa cuando estoy viéndote dormir. Permíteme acariciarte tu mejilla y cantarte muy suabe una canción en el oíd ...

My eyes fluttered open because I could hear Ricarito calling me from his bed. He slept just on the other side of the wall. From his birth, even his slightest sigh could pull me from a deep sleep and compel me to go check on him. In the mental mists between slumber and wake, I tiptoed to Ricky's room. Silently slipping in and closing the door behind me, I once again allowed myself to crawl into his bed so I could hold him close during these last few minutes of the night's rest. It was during these moments that our hearts were knit together as tightly as they could be, and my joy as his mother knew no bounds. The warmth of his little body so relaxed in my arms always brought me to the bliss of pure love that God must feel for us.

But the sheets were cold. The pillow did not hold his scent. As the shadows moved in thicker and tears welled from my soul, I yet again surrendered to the waking nightmare that had become my life. Ricardo's bed was empty.

In June 1998, I sat beside my husband of 12 years watching him take his last breaths. At the urging of my parents, I had married Bernardo when I was 18. Before then, I had dreamed of travel and education, but my family had made it clear that Bernardo's social status and secure financial position would help everyone in my family. I owed it to my younger siblings to settle into the predictable life of an Argentine mother. I bore him two sons, gracefully attended to our comfortable home and social life, but never truly loved Bernardo a day.

My father always said he didn't understand where my discontent could be coming from. I had lived a good life, a proper life, surrounded by a large and loving family. My siblings and I had attended the private Catholic school in my town, even though my family needed to live modestly so we could afford it. When I met Bernardo, he was 10 years my senior and already a well-established businessman in our community. Everyone agreed we were a good match.

His parents did not mind that my family brought little social or political benefit to them. They were pleased that their son appeared to be in love, was financially stable and comfortable, and had a beautiful, fruitful wife. My life's goal and purpose, as had been defined by my Argentinian culture long before I was born, was complete.

Now, at 30 years old, I sat beside Bernardo as he suffered through his last days of cancer and wondered what would become of me.

I knew I should be ashamed that I felt like a caged animal restlessly pacing at the door of my husband's death. Our two sons sat on the other side of the room quietly teasing each other. They were blissfully ignorant of the tsunami of change that was rushing toward them. Their father had been so ill for so long that they could not remember him any other way. Marco, the eldest at 11 years old, was smart, handsome, and had taken on many of the social responsibilities of being the man of the house for last five years. He had accompanied me to church, the bank, and the few social gatherings I attended—things a husband was normally expected to do. Ricardo was seven years old and had the heart of an adventurer. For him, everything in life was either a daring quest or an unbearable bore. Sitting still or being quiet was just not possible for Ricardo.

I heard a small choke and then a deep exhale from the bed. I squeezed my eyes shut, not wanting to have my last vision of Bernardo be his body's reflexive fight to live even though his soul had left. At that moment, I sensed my husband's palm caress my cheek, and I tilted my head to press into it. Tears began to stream down my face, splashing onto my tightly folded hands. He had loved me truly, and I understood that in this last good-bye he wished me every happiness. Suddenly it occurred to me that in the mystic realm of the unknowable, Bernardo's unrequited love for me might have actually been the source of his illness. His letting go of life may have been his ultimate gift to me. He had offered me a second chance at having a life I could truly call my own.

The days and then months after Bernardo's death had raced past me. Everyone seemed to have an opinion about how I should move forward. I was grateful that both my boys had school to go to. It gave them a routine that someone other than I was responsible for. Surrounded by their friends, they quickly returned to their normal day-to-day activities. But for me, it was harder. I had been Bernardo's caregiver for a very long time. Now that I didn't have medications to administer or bedpans to empty, I was having a hard time figuring out what to do with myself. Bernardo had left me enough money that our sons and I could live comfortably.

A whole year went by before the gray haze finally began to lift.

I longed to go somewhere new and start over. If I stayed in my town, I would never be more than Bernardo Romero's widow, not Rosa Angelina Estrada Romero, the independent and strong woman I wanted to be. But where could I go? If I moved away, I would most likely have to work. I prayed for guidance.

I talked to my parents, but they couldn't empathize with my ambition for autonomy. They were also getting older, and it made perfect sense for me to settle in and plan on being their caregiver when the time came. My siblings, who were married with families of their own, all agreed that I should just manage my savings carefully and protect my comfortable, quiet life from change. For them, the predictability and security of my days was something to be envied.

Only my friend, Lucilla, understood what was in my heart. She and I had grown up together and spent many, many afternoons lying on the grass in her parents' courtyard, telling each other our deepest thoughts. She admitted that she had witnessed me die inside when I married and knew I was a caged bird that needed to be freed.

It was Lucilla who put in my head that I should go to the United States. And once it was in my head, the idea took over every moment of the day and night. I should live in America. Nothing would stop me from making that a reality, but there was no clear path to set out on. I waited for God to show me how to begin.

Soon the spirit moved. Lucilla put out inquiries to everyone we knew asking if anyone had friends or relatives who had moved to the United States. Argentinians are wonderful that way—we consider it an honor to be asked for help. In just a few days, Lucilla made contact with an elementary school classmate, Marianna Alvarez. Her family had moved to Salt Lake City almost 20 years prior after converting to Mormonism. At the time, it had been the talk of the whole town—someone left the Catholic Church and then left Argentina. It was unheard of. But everyone wished them well—after all, a person is an Argentinian forever whether she likes it or not, but a member of a religion only as long as she feels it is right for her.

In just a few short weeks, arrangements had been made for my sons and me to travel to Utah and stay with the Alvarezes until we were on our feet. I had the breath of the angels under my wings, and I felt strong and confident as I pulled my plans together ... until Marco drew his line in the sand.

While I had been living in a fog for the past two years, Marco had grown up. I was shocked when I finally looked at my eldest son with new eyes and saw a young man standing there. When had he stopped being my baby? When had he come to realize that he had a life of his own to live? Now in his early teens, Marco was already clear about his future: he would attend the University of Buenos Aires and study to become a doctor. He was determined to find a cure to the tortuous disease that had taken his father from him. Then it hit me—Marco lived through the declining health and untimely death of his father in an entirely different reality than I had. As a growing child, he was forced to stand by helplessly and watch the man he most loved and admired wither away before his eyes. I always assumed that my children could not possibly be cognizant of, or deeply affected by, Bernardo's suffering. I was wrong. Marco was shaped by it and would not shrink from the regret and responsibility he had come to feel.

Marco's decision took the wind out of my sails. While my parents gladly offered to have him live with them, how could I leave my son? Like Abraham and Isaac, I felt I was being unfairly tested. Is a mother's life valued less than her children's? Should I let my dream go like a balloon in the wind so I could fulfill what nearly every culture on earth told me was my God-given duty? Could I survive the sorrow of leaving Marco behind?

Again, I prayed, and soon the answer came, bright and clear and unmistakable. While a large part of my soul would stay in Argentina with Marco, Ricardo and I would to go to Utah. To do otherwise would be to teach my children that being true to their inner voices was only a nice idea, not each person's divine guidance to his or her personal purpose in life, which I sincerely believed. I would not let my boys down like that. My greatest gift to them was teaching them that their autonomy was a birthright that should never be set aside for anyone or anything.

On the morning Ricardo and I were at the airport ready to leave for Salt Lake City, I was inspired by a graffiti quote that my angels had obviously put there for me to read: "Leap and the net will appear." It became my guiding principle over the following months.

The Alvarez family welcomed us in warm Argentinian fashion. Ricardo and I shared a comfortable bedroom that one of their children had vacated for us. We were added to the dining room table as though we had always been there. An entire Latin community went into motion to make sure Ricardo was enrolled in school, I had work, we had opportunities to make friends, and that Salt Lake would not feel too foreign to us for too long. They put us in touch with a lawyer who specialized in immigration issues and would allow me to pay him in installments once I found work.

My temporary work visa came through quickly, and within six months we were renting our own home and settling into our new life. I had a job with *Amiga's*

Cleaning—a woman-owned and operated house cleaning service with clients all over northern Utah. The owner, Monica Morales, became my role model. She was strong, yet feminine, and sharp as a tack. Her staff became my friends and support squad. They were as loyal and protective of one another as a band of soldiers. This *tour-de-force* of women embraced me, and soon I grew to love them. This was exactly what I had dreamed of—strong women having lives and money of their own. This never could have happened in my hometown.

It took four years for Ricardo and me to attain our full US citizenship. It was a long, difficult road, but we were so well taken care of by our Latin community that we never felt alone or far from home. It would take a few more years, but I knew exactly what I wanted to do with my new life: own a business of my own so I could help women the same way I had been helped.

The next decade raced by in a blur. It seemed that one day, Ricardo was nine years old and struggling to learn English, and the next I was attending his high school graduation. He had grown up to be a kind, wonderful man with dreams of being a doctor like his brother. We had not been financially able to go back to Argentina to see Marco or my family, and they had never been to visit us either. I suppose they still felt as though I had deserted them. Ricardo and I promised each other that we would take a month to visit Argentina after his college graduation, which was only months away.

My cleaning business grew steadily over the years, and eventually I had many people working for me who were in the same set of circumstances as I had been when I first came to the Utah. I had even met a man I felt I could love. I expanded the business beyond residential cleaning and now had many owners of large office buildings as my clients.

Bill owned a large building downtown and contacted me for a bid. It was my practice to never just e-mail a bid; I always insisted on hand-delivering it so I could size up who I might be doing business with. I had become one tough cookie, as they say. However, Bill was a romantic through and through. He fell in love with me at first sight and wooed me like I was a queen. It took him a long time to get through my tough exterior, but once he did, we were both head over heels for each other. How wonderful it was to fall in love for the first time at an age when I could fully grasp the wondrous gift it is.

One of my great joys was singing in my church's choir. Ricardo and I met so many wonderful people there that hardly a day went by that we weren't there for one thing or another. Bill wasn't Latin or Catholic, but he joined us all the same and learned to love it, too. It was when I was singing that I felt most close to God, most joyful, and free of worry. Soon I found myself singing all the time—by myself while I worked, with Ricardo when we were in the car, with Bill when we were having dinner. The melodies were always there, waiting to come out and fully express my feelings.

I'll never forget the song the three of us were singing together over lunch that day. Bill, Ricardo, and I were sitting down to steamy bowls of *pazzole* because the gray

November skies chilled us all to the bone. Ricardo was feeling silly and began to hum Abba's "Gimme! Gimme! Gimme!" and soon Bill and I burst in with the lyrics. All of us loved Abba because we knew the words so well.

At the end, we clinked glasses to toast our performances. An hour later, I needed to leave for work, and Ricardo needed to go to the University's library to study. We lived just 20 minutes from the school, so I had bought him a little beat-up Toyota truck to drive back and forth. We kissed, we hugged, and we said we would see each other at seven o'clock for dinner.

*   *   *   *   *   *   *   *   *   *

I was getting mad. It was eight-thirty, dinner had come and gone, and Ricardo was nowhere to be seen and hadn't called. This wasn't typical, but it also wasn't the first time. After all, he was a teenager, and his friends (particularly girlfriends) often made him forget anything he promised me. Only the week before he hadn't come home until after midnight because he'd been playing pool with some classmates. I did my best to not scold him too often. His grades were near perfect, I never worried about him drinking and driving, and he hated drugs even more than I did. I cleared the table and went to bed. I was tired, and I knew he'd tell me what had happened at breakfast.

I had an early appointment the next morning and needed to eat and run. I let Ricardo sleep in since I knew he'd been out late the night before. Just as I was leaving the house, I cracked open his bedroom door to ask him to call me when he got up. It is that moment, those lifelong five seconds, that I remember more than any other. Standing in the doorway, staring at an empty bed, every sense in my body and soul shuddered. I tried to buoy myself with reasonable explanations, but I knew in the way that only a mother can that something was terribly wrong. Even if he had been caught up in the rapture of love, Ricardo would have called. My vision blurred, my stomach retched, my knees buckled.

I thought I had known courage. I thought I was tough. But the courage and toughness I had to muster in order to dial 911 has never again been matched. I can't remember how Bill found out, but he was there when the police came.

I can't remember anything that happened that week except paperwork and odd questions from investigators. I didn't sleep or eat or even cry. I just sat waiting for Ricardo to come home. I was afraid that if I left the house, he would try to find me, but wouldn't be able to. I was afraid if I closed my eyes, his sixth sense would be reaching for mine, and I wouldn't know. My heart scanned the sky, my soul searched the voids, my mind pleaded with him to come back to me. I never heard his voice again except in my dreams.

Over a year passed before a wandering sheep farmer found the little beat-up Toyota in a desolate part of Wyoming. Some miles away, investigators found a young man's skull that had been crushed with a heavy object. There were no clues that filled in any details.

Now, almost a decade later, I still search for Ricardo with my heart. Sometimes he answers me; a few times he's sat beside me. I've tried so many times to imagine the horror of his last day of life, but fear is never what he communicates to me. What he sends me is peace and joy and gratitude. These are with me as his gifts, always. However, I have never allowed myself to sing even a single note again.

In his memory, I will continue to live one moment at a time and smile at everyone I meet.

Appendix
The 100 Answers to Each Survey Question

1: How Would You Define Courage?

1. Trust.
2. Courage to me is being true to myself in body, mind and spirit; not allowing others to dictate what is in my best interest.
3. Raised Catholic, I was taught that caring for others was my number one job and that humility was mandatory. Being true to myself was never taught because my job in life was to care for people less fortunate than myself. It took me years to find my voice, and to express the spirit within me. In essence, this does help those less fortunate than myself because I can share the joy within me with others.
4. I rely on Angeles Arrien's definition, which is to stand by my heart. I also like the characterization of courage as not the absence of fear, but perseverance despite fear.
5. The ability to stand up with one's convictions in the face of danger, threat, bullying, or injustice.

The strength to face down wrong with right in defense of self or the defenseless.

6. Bravery and positive action in the face of overwhelming obstacles.

7. Mental or moral strength to face life's deepest fears and most difficult times. It is the ability to go forward despite the obstacles.

8. Courage is being able to carry the weight of the world on your shoulders and still cook dinner for your family with a smile.

9. The willingness to face your fears and be vulnerable and take a risk.

10. The ability to move forward each day no matter what has knocked you down the day before.

11. The ability to do what moves you under any circumstance, to right a wrong, to stand up alone against the odds and make a difference. Sometimes just being a woman takes courage.

12. By not becoming paralyzed, even when the conditions are not good.

13. The ability to take a stand for whatever you believe in.

14. The ability to step far outside your comfort zone, to push forward in life even when you doubt you can. Sometimes it's just doing what needs to be done, even (or especially) when you would rather not. It can be trusting that tomorrow will be a better day, or simply believing in yourself in the face of life's most challenging moments.

15. True courage is the ability to find a rainbow when darkness surrounds.
16. Having a broad set of shoulders to carry everything good and bad that comes along in our lives. Keeping a positive attitude!
17. The ability to move forward in the face of adversity.
18. I define courage as the wisdom and strength of will to follow my path, even when shortcuts/deviations may prove easier.
19. Courage is being able to feel the helplessness in a situation and to know that in my weakness is the strength to come through it. To know that a difficult situation is not against me, but for me, and to know that this too shall pass.
20. Taking that step when there's a hesitation or fear that rests inside. Taking it despite having that piece of you that wants to pull you back so you can remain in a safe and familiar place, but you take that step anyway to do what you know you must do.
21. Being able to face challenging times in life.
22. The ability to speak or act in a manner far beyond one's comfort zone. Facing adversity or challenge without deferring to its power.
23. Pushing past my fear. It is something inside of me that helps me find my voice when I stand up.
24. Moving forward in spite of past failures, hurts, and fears. Asking others for help. Showing up and being present when there is no obvious reward.

25. Giving to others what we most want from them, even when we feel most deprived.

26. A willingness to do what challenges and scares me. A willingness to be honest, first with myself, and then to speak my truth to power (both institutional and personal) in the face of apathy and "go-along-ism."

27. The ability to stand up for your convictions and not cave even when it is so very hard.

28. Never losing myself.

29. Inner strength to move forward despite challenges.

30. That deepest part of one's soul that knows and believes in one's self. To be able to pick yourself up in the most difficult of situations. To keep going because we know and believe that what we're here to do is bigger than anyone or anything that can knock us down.

31. Courage is the ability to face adversity head-on. Courage is taking personal responsibility for your own life.

32. The willingness to think openly without fear of ridicule. To walk outside the lines for a bigger view of our universe. To walk down a path without fear of what may be found … trusting the not-yet-known. If the universe sends you a message, listen and act!

33. Courage is putting all fears of the past behind and moving forward with a deep knowing that faith and hope are going to hold me up.

34. Courage is diving into the unknown without certainty of the outcome, but with certainty of the learning possibilities.

35. The ability to take on things that are challenging and not put them off because they are unfamiliar or risky.

36. Courage is the choice to overcome what seems like an impossible obstacle. This can happen in both very small and very large ways in life. Every moment we are making courageous choices.

37. Having the strength to keep going no matter what.

38. Facing fear is one of the hardest things to do. So many things that happen in life scare us into second-guessing our worth and our abilities. It takes courage to face those fears head-on and do the best we can with what we have.

39. Being able to overcome any obstacle with your head held high.

40. Courage is actually doing something when your mind, body, and heart may not agree. You have to confront your greatest fears and go forth with confidence.

41. Inner strength to take on anything in front of you. I give my parents credit for having the courage to give their children the life they could not have in their homeland.

42. Courage is being afraid and doing it anyway!

43. Courageous people see tribulation and reach within themselves to find the anchor that holds

them together. Quite often, for myself, that anchor has been my children. I am a stronger, wiser, more flexible person because of my children. I can honestly look back over their lives and see where I've grown, where I've become stronger and more resilient.

44. Taking a big swallow, ignoring what is frightening you, and walking straight toward what needs to be done.

45. Courage is taking risks; taking a big leap of faith into the unknown because you want more out of your life, and you're not willing to settle for just okay.

46. Courage is traveling to, loving, hurting, feeling, and fighting for the life that you picture for yourself. Never settling for something that simply leaves you satisfied and content. Courage is taking a leap of faith because you never want life to be merely satisfactory; you want it to be amazing.

47. Courage is taking risks and standing up for what you believe in.

48. I like Hemmingway's definition: "Grace under pressure." There have been times in my life when I haven't withstood danger, fear, and difficulty; instead, I've crumpled completely. Does that mean I didn't have courage? Hardly. I had the courage to feel my feelings and keep breathing. But considering what I've faced, how have I done this? That's where the grace comes in.

49. The strength from within to do something you find slightly scary.

50. Courage is being honest about who you are.

51. Courage is doing something out of your comfort zone, whether that's physically, mentally, or being of service to others.

52. Courage is accepting and wanting to learn about all types of peoples and cultures, taking their knowledge and embracing our differences.

53. Courage is having the will to act and perform outside you comfort level.

54. The ability to dig even deeper than you thought you could so you can do what is in front of you.

55. Courage is facing adversity with optimism, resolve, and fearlessness. To have the belief in yourself to face full-on the reality of the situation.

56. Strength in your convictions. Being brave in the face of difficulty. Having the will to carry on when faced with challenges that are sometimes beyond your control. Being able to overcome your fear to persevere and tackle any situation that may come your way; remaining strong.

57. The ability to face and carry on after major life-changing events.

58. Courage is making a conscious decision to maintain a passion for life after facing its adversities.

59. Courage and strength, even when you don't feel you have it, to do not only what needs to be done, but also to do what you want for yourself

and others. To go against the odds, or others' perceptions, to accomplish something. Courage is facing fear, accepting that you may lose, but being willing to try anyway

60. The ability to deal with the scary times; not just the physical challenges, but also the emotional ones. Often times those are much more scary!

61. When you stand up for what is right, whether verbally or with actions. If something makes you a little nervous, or you have to muster up the energy for days to do it, that is courage, and it is powerful. Moving forward against adversity.

62. To conquer fear. To live through an ordeal or crisis and come out a stronger person.

63. Defending your beliefs. Protecting yourself and others against those who oppose your beliefs, or seek to harm you or others, even if your defense creates a bodily risk to you or a risk to your relationship with others.

64. Standing up for your values and moral beliefs even when public opinion or others belittle those values, or they are unpopular.

65. Finding an inner strength that you may not have ever known was inside you. Yet when it is needed to protect yourself or someone else, it comes out.

66. Courage is the ability to face fears and move ahead anyway.

67. Courage is the ability to forge ahead regardless of your level of fear.

68. A person being able to pull herself up against all odds. This type of courage simply makes for a much better person, even though the thought of going through something horrible would never be her choice.

69. Sitting still with what you fear and then going forward with it anyway.

70. Proceeding with your plans in the face of fear.

71. Courage is to feel the fear and do it anyhow.

72. The strength to do what is right. The ability to take risks. Being self-confident and trusting in yourself.

73. Courage is to find the strength to deal with adversity. Courage is also to recognize when you have hit rock bottom, take the time to accept that, and then summon the courage and strength to slowly start moving away from that dark place.

74. Courage is facing your fears one tiny inhalation of breath at a time.

75. Doing what needs to be done no matter how fearful one feels. But choice needs to be involved in the act of courage. Where there is no choice, there is no courage.

76. Having the strength to continue on, even with fears, anxiety, and doubts. Leaving your comfort zone.

77. Having the ability to stand and face adversity, fear, change, uncertainty, and challenges with confidence, strength, and wisdom.

78. The ability to stand for truth and dignity when all others are working against you.

79. Overcoming obstacles with a positive attitude.

80. Doing things that you know you need to do, but for some reason you're afraid or don't want to do them.

81. Facing an unexpected challenge that could define or change the rest of your life.

82. Courage is grace under pressure. Doing what needs to be done in spite of fear or obstacles.

83. Courage is the ability to walk in this world with your head held high and share your unique gifts. Sometimes it takes a lifetime to demonstrate this; I know it has taken me a great many years. However, true courage is gathering the strength to outshine the worst darkness when it enters into your life and threatens your very being or that of your family.

84. Courage is having the strength to do something you know you need to do, even if you don't know how to do it.

85. Courage is not letting anything, like fear or failure, hold you back from doing something.

86. Courage is not being fearless. It is feeling fear and pushing through it because the cause is worth it.

87. To face a daunting and difficult situation with strength and fortitude.

88. Courage: the mental strength and firm determination to achieve and persevere hardship

with stubborn persistence. (I admit that I needed *Webster's* to find the correct wording.)

89. The ability to enter a new space, either physically or emotionally. To me, it is where you're at risk of getting hurt, but instead *choose* to do something that you would not typically do.

90. To have strength to do something that you would normally doubt first.

91. Courage is the conscious decision to pick up our fears like a suitcase and take them with us on the trip of life. I don't think we can truly conquer our fears, but only become comfortable with their presence and then keep moving. The real trick is to learn to hear the difference between our inner voice and our fears.

92. The willingness to stick something out to the end, no matter the circumstances.

93. Courage is facing our fears.

94. The willingness to put yourself out there, even if you might fail, and/or the tenacity to fight through anything with passion, heart, empathy, and determination, no matter how difficult.

95. Having the inner strength to never give up. When life knocks you down, don't sit in self-pity for too long. Jump up and give it another try!

96. I define courage as not how one would react to a situation that poses danger, but how one would continue on in life afterward. Courage is when someone gets up every day and does the right thing, not for validation, but for self-fulfillment.

97. Courage is the ability to see the big picture and strive for it, but not succumb to issues of pride.
98. Courage is to sometimes be silent and do nothing, think and not react, and pick and choose my battles.
99. Courage is to step out of my comfort zone to improve.
100. The ability to follow your heart or your gut instinct about what is right for you.

2: Have You Had the Opportunity to Demonstrate Courage?

1. Yes, with my career. I'm trained as a chef and demonstrate courage everyday. I started my own business and learned to navigate those unknown waters.
2. Joining Toastmasters was a demonstration of personal courage, to find and express my voice. At my second meeting I approached a professional speaker in the group and asked him to be my mentor. That decision showed extra special courage. I knew I needed help to stand behind that lectern and deliver dynamic speeches. With my mentor's help, I worked very hard to learn how to write and deliver speeches. This experience showed tremendous courage within me. Together we achieved so much more than I could have done alone.

3.   I learned to competitively race a vintage Porsche racecar and raced at many legendary tracks in the United States. Going to a professional race school at the Laguna Seca Raceway in California showed tremendous courage inside me. I learned that fear and excitement are the same neuron-pathway within the body, so I told myself the fear I felt was really excitement. That took courage.

4.   The first few times I went in front of a live audience in the role of Eva Peron in Evita took every ounce of courage I had. I still have actor's nightmares about that two-plus years later.

5.   Working for Goldman Sachs took courage. As an outside consultant, the clients took pleasure in torturing me and trying to make me cry. I am not kidding. I spent a lot of time crying in the bathroom.

6.   I left my first husband for another man, which is the most courageous thing I have ever done.

7.   Yes. Once, when a large group of men were telling very degrading jokes about women, I actually stood up in the group of 110 and told them it was neither funny nor okay. They booed.

8.   On many occasions.

9.   Taking a new career and having to learn a new skill beyond my comfort zone.

10. Yes, when I had my second baby at only 23 weeks and helped him live.

11. I believe that any situation that requires a person to grow and expand is an opportunity to demonstrate courage.

12. Yes, when I have lost close loved ones after watching them suffer through illness and despair. But I held the belief that you must be present, you must be compassionate, and love them through the fear and pain of losing. It's not that you pretend they are not dying, but you try to work through and validate your love while comforting them and communicating all you can, knowing that life will never be the same once they are gone.

13. I lost my first child at nine months old, and my third child (who is now almost 40) has cerebral palsy. He has been a Special Education teacher for 15 years, teacher of the year almost every year, and is just a gift from God!

14. Plenty of times. Most recently while undergoing breast cancer treatment and standing my ground against irate plastic surgeons and oncologists!

15. Going through several Army development, leadership, and training schools, I have had many opportunities to demonstrate courage. I remember on my first jump out of an airplane during Airborne School, there must have been 30 of us lined up to go, and I was the first one. I had to stare outside the door, knowing I would put my foot into thin air and fall, waiting the long three one-thousand counts and hoping to

feel that chute open. I was a second lieutenant, five foot five inches tall, trying to act strong, yet experiencing uncertainty in everything I did.

16. I had worked in an organization for a long time when my career there was coming to an end. During the last few months, a person was brought in to replace me whose character was highly questionable. I was tempted to sit still, wait it out, and just move on. But I could not leave my team with someone whom I did not respect. I had nothing to gain and a lot to lose by talking to my boss before I left, but I did. I now feel that practicing that kind of courage on a regular basis is what makes it a fundamental part of your character.

17. Not so far. I do not look forward to this time, as I know it is extremely demanding of one's mind and feelings of stability or well-being.

18. I moved to the United States from Russia all alone when I was only 25. I soon found myself in an abusive marriage with a young son. One day, I left with only my son and nothing else. As I hid from my abusive husband, we stayed in a shelter for three months and could not tell anyone where I was.

19. I am 68 years old and proud to say I have demonstrated courage many times in my life. I was always surprised at my strength. Every challenge I met taught me something new about myself.

20. I demonstrate courage when I take a stance that is not necessarily popular with others just to make a point or to stand for an important belief or value.

21. I demonstrate courage in my own home every time I suggest something to my husband or kids that I know they are not going respond well to. I courageously speak and listen.

22. I feel like I constantly put myself out there as a trainer, speaker, and author, even though I never feel completely confident. It takes courage to keep moving forward like this.

23. I'm often courageous when I push myself to expand my capacities.

24. It has taken a lot of courage to survive the American culture without marrying until I was 50 and never having children.

25. I have been a performer my whole adult life, even though I often battle depression and have an introverted disposition. That's taken a lot of courage.

26. When I lost both my father and my husband close together. It was so hard to keep going.

27. When I got divorced, it took so much courage to sell my home and move into a mobile home.

28. I faced and beat cancer.

29. When I left a very controlling husband, I stood up for myself, and my daughters, against his whole family.

30. There have been many times that men in powerful positions have tried to overwhelm me with decisions regarding my children and their welfare. I can honestly say that I have never backed down.

31. When I finally left an abusive relationship and began my own career from scratch.

32. I feel like I challenge myself to get out of my comfort zone. Traveling by myself, moving to a new state, and meeting new people by myself made me so uncomfortable. But each risk I took brought me something in the way of a lesson, friend, experience, or story.

33. My past relationship was very abusive, but I had to take the risk to leave or perhaps be killed.

34. My father died when I was 13, and it felt like I lost my mom that year, too, because she started drinking heavily.

35. I was captured by a cult when I was 19 and held against my will at one of their communes. I ran away, with their leaders in hot pursuit. I finally got a police escort home.

36. My only son, whom I love more than anything in the world, suffers from schizophrenia and is too paranoid to seek help. I don't know where or how he lives; he hides from his family. Not knowing how to help him is taking more courage than I may have.

37. Raising my four children in a home with an active alcoholic is taking a great deal of courage. I do

not want to abandon the husband I have loved because he is in pain.

38. My husband has been chronically ill for over 20 years.

39. When my husband lost his business, it took a great deal of courage to keep my head up in public.

40. When we were still very young, my husband died in a plane crash, and I could not imagine how I would raise our children without him.

41. My older sister committed suicide, and I've raised her children.

42. Two of my three daughters had breast cancer, and I cared for them through their treatment. One lived, but the other did not.

43. I had many awful things happen to me, but sometimes I think it takes as much courage to get out of bed in the morning during a rough week as it does to care for a dying child.

44. When my sister was admitted to a mental hospital, I had to be very courageous to support my parents so they didn't collapse from the sorrow.

45. I feel like every time I enter into an intimate relationship, I demonstrate a lot of courage. I was sexually abused as a child.

46. Following the feeling inside me that says I deserve better than an abusive relationship is taking a lot of courage.

47. When I was publically betrayed and humiliated by people I thought were my friends, it took a lot of courage to come back from that very dark place and learn to trust people again.

48. The first time I completed a running race took a great deal of courage.

49. After losing a business, I opened another one despite my fears.

50. Because of his overconsumption of alcohol, my dad was in and out of ICUs many, many times over five years. It was awful for my whole family.

51. I suffer from chronic fatigue and often become overwhelmed and depressed. It takes a lot to pick myself back up and keep going.

52. I find it is all the small things, like really listening to my husband or not yelling at my kids that add up to courage.

53. I called off my wedding at the last minute because I knew it just wasn't right for me.

54. I think I am better at being courageous in the face of physical threats than emotional ones. I don't have nearly as much anxiety when whitewater rafting or rock climbing or driving in a snowstorm as I do when I need to confront a loved one.

55. Leaving a 20-year-long relationship took courage.

56. I have the courage to tell others who I know do not respect my religion that I am a practicing Christian.

57. I work with immigrant children, and it takes a great deal of courage to tell ignorant people that

their bigotry is part of the problem. I don't think immigrants are a problem. They are part of the solution.

58. I believe that animals are sentient beings and refuse to be complicit in their abuse by humans.

59. Just surviving takes courage!

60. Trying to let go of the past and look into the blank future.

61. Admitting when I'm wrong takes a lot of courage.

62. I had a baby when I was a teenager, and all the grownups around me said I'd blown my chances and would never go to college. Today, I'm the proud mom of that baby *and* I have a PhD! Ha! Take that!

63. It takes courage to take on any assignment that doesn't guarantee success; that applies to jobs, relationships, and especially raising children.

64. I survived a 28-year marriage in which I was maritally raped for the last several years. I ran with only my pajamas and keys, but I've made it.

65. Reevaluating my relationship with my kids and husband so that it works for me, too, has taken a lot of courage.

66. I went into business with my husband even though everyone told us what a bad idea that was and that we'd never last. It's been 18 great years now!

67. Completing my first triathlon at 50.

68. Not marrying my high school boyfriend, even though that was what everyone expected of me.

69. I left a 27-year-long marriage with no career, no emotional support, and no money.

70. When my daughter was only 10 years old, she got cancer. Helping her through this took more courage than I thought I had.

71. Women demonstrate courage every time they reach to become better mothers, better people, more self-sufficient.

72. As a teacher, I demonstrate courage every day by putting up with crap in the field of education just so I can pursue my love of teaching kids.

73. Just after I had my youngest child and was in the midst of a divorce, my doctor told me I had three months left to live. That was several years ago, and it still chills me to the bone.

74. Leaving my job of 18 years to be a stay-at-home mom.

75. When I found out my oldest child was addicted to heroin.

76. I have often had to stand up for what I alone believed was true. But to do otherwise would have meant I was a coward.

77. When my husband and I had to declare bankruptcy after having been quite wealthy. The public humiliation was horrible.

78. My father committed suicide, and my mother became an alcoholic because of it.

79. Letting my child walk her journey and take her own risks is one of the hardest things I have ever

had to do. She became addicted to drugs, and she had to find her own way out of it.

80. Quitting my full-time job and starting my own business has taken a lot of courage.

81. When I need courage, I look at a pewter brick I have with this quote, "What would you do if you knew you could not fail?" That always inspires me and gets me going again.

82. Getting through college took a lot of courage for me. There were many, many obstacles.

83. When I had to put my mom in a nursing home. She had Alzheimer's and hated me for not being able to take care of her myself.

84. Letting my son quit college. I'm so worried about his future, but I have to let him live his own life.

85. It has taken so much courage to leave a marriage that was so unfulfilling, even though my kids begged me not to. I wonder if I'll ever get over the guilt of drastically changing their lives just to make my own better.

86. I stayed in a physically abusive relationship for years because it legally helped me keep custody of my daughter from a previous marriage.

87. I live in a town where everyone seems so rich, but I only make 15 dollars an hour. It takes courage to hold my head up.

88. It takes courage to stand up to a boss who expects me to sell things to people who can't afford them.

89. It took a lot of courage to be an attractive woman in the army. But it was so worth it!

90. Every time I sign into my Match.com account, I need to muster my courage.

91. I work in a women's shelter, and facing women and their children who are scared and abused takes all the courage I have. Sometimes I just can't go to work.

92. After years of raising children and being out of the workforce, my husband left me. I had to take a job as a housekeeper in a hotel. It took courage to give up my self-image and do what had to be done.

93. Being turned down by the university I wanted to go to was hard. It took courage to apply to others until I got into one.

94. Getting on stage in front of a lot of people for the first time took a lot of courage, but I loved it!

95. I had to confront my child's teacher about how she was treating him in class. I was so afraid to be labeled a whiny mom, but you have to stand up for your kids, right?

96. Sending my son to school in Europe took so much courage. I knew it would be great for him, but seeing that plane take off almost did me in.

97. Holding my head up and moving forward after I was fired from a job I'd held for nearly 20 years.

98. Facing my fears about making a fool of myself in front of others has taken courage. I've had to get through second-guessing myself and just move forward.

99. Severing the relationship with my mother, who was always verbally abusive, has taken a lot of courage. I think there is no reason to stay in any relationship that pulls you down all the time.

100. Giving up opportunities that I really wanted so I could finish raising my children has taken courage. I have to believe they [the opportunities] will come around again someday.

3: Was There a Defining Moment in Your Life That Made You Who You Are Today?

1. Becoming a mother.

2. At 12 years old, the hospital called our house and told my mom and me that my dad had died in surgery. I ran up to his room to look for something—a watch, a shirt, anything that I could hold so I felt connected to my dad. Then a voice from inside me said, *My dad will always be with me.* That defining moment is still with me.

3. The first time I stood up to my alcoholic, abusive husband. I didn't know I had it in me, but I'm glad I found it.

4. When I became pregnant at 17.

5. When I realized that education was the most important tool I could acquire.

6. When I had to attend my child's kindergarten teacher conference from a hotel in a different state. It was then that I realized I had to make a change and be available for my kids, my husband,

my parents, and my kid's teachers while making an income.

7. No.

8. In the third grade, a very mean teacher told my mom I needed to be in class with the "retarded" kids. That may have saved me, because I found the "retards" to be much more kind than the other kids or faculty at that school. Although I was in that group for only six months before they decided that, in fact, I was normal, it gave me compassion for others that has defined my whole life.

9. I've had a lot of defining moments, not just one.

10. Only three weeks after my college graduation, I was in the USMC Officer Candidate School in Virginia. This training changed the trajectory of my life forever, shaping me and giving me confidence I did not have before.

11. In the fourth grade, I realized that it was all going to be up to me, that no one would be supporting me. It would all be on my shoulders.

12. When I was six years old, my dad died suddenly. For the rest of my life I have been driven to succeed so I wouldn't be left with limited options like my mom was.

13. When my baby had to spend four months in the hospital. I realized then what really matters.

14. The night I left the husband who had been maritally raping me for several years.

15. When I figured out I could do anything I set my mind to.
16. When I forgave my parents for not doing a better job. I stopped being afraid to become a parent myself.
17. When my babies were sick, a physical therapist told me not to worry about the future, but to take one step at a time. That is now my life motto.
18. My divorce.
19. Being told I had a very aggressive, rare breast cancer tumor: my whole world and my attitude toward it flipped in that single moment.
20. At the height of my professional practice as a therapist, my daughter took her own life. I experienced deep depression, but also found a higher power that helps me to this day.
21. When I realized that when I set goals and focused on them, I could make them happen.
22. No.
23. Having an alcoholic father.
24. When I found out my husband was having an affair.
25. The illness and death of my mother at an early age.
26. When I left my alcoholic and abusive husband.
27. Discovering the amazing concept of pivot points; those moments in life that put you on a different path due to a conscious change you make.
28. When, at 36, I lost my husband in a tragic accident. My two small children and I had to move in with my parents.

29. As a child, my family left me in India. At first I was terrified, but then I realized I would be free from their constant negativity and criticism.

30. Having the courage and determination to take responsibility for a huge health issue. I took charge of my care and enlisted my surgeon, and others, to act in my best interest.

31. When I made it through community college while raising my children.

32. I took a seminar series in the early nineties called Education for Living. The teachings and opportunities to practice them fundamentally changed my way of being.

33. Meeting and marrying my life partner. I never thought I would experience this joy in my lifetime.

34. Not a moment, but a theme has run throughout my life. I grew up in a very conservative, Catholic family that would not let me do many things, because I was a girl and needed to be sheltered. I left my family because of this, and now I never hesitate to do anything I enjoy just because I am a woman.

35. The sudden death of my husband changed everything.

36. My amazing journey started the day my ex-husband left me. For a while, I was in deep, dark places, but later I realized it was the best thing he ever did for me.

37. When I overcame my drug addiction.

38. When I went back to school to complete my education.

39. When my husband had a terrible accident. We had to reverse roles. I became the breadwinner and he became Mr. Mom.

40. Not just one, but very, very many.

41. Arriving in a whole new country where I had to find the courage and confidence to fit in and do my best to accomplish all the work.

42. July 25, 19**. Before that defining moment, my life was at the mercy of my alcoholism. I got sober, and it was a life-changer.

43. Maybe not a moment, but having children has defined me. They have made me reevaluate my career decisions, where we live, and how we choose to spend our time.

44. When I retired from a career in education after 23 years and took on a new career.

45. When I decided that I, too, deserved a life and happiness.

46. After I lost my parents at a very early age, I lost my infant son. The day I realized I was strong enough to move on without pity was a defining moment.

47. I do not think there was just one. I think it was a build-up of all those major events that has shown me what I am made of.

48. I don't believe in defining moments. I think how you act on a daily basis is what defines you.

49. Working two jobs since I was 15 made me independent and taught me how to handle life.

50. No.

51. After a relationship ended poorly, I emptied a bottle of pills, wanting everything to end. When I learned what people had done for me to bring me back, I was humiliated that I didn't succeed. But two women I worked with insisted I get professional help. The defining moment was when I realized that these women thought I was worth helping.

52. I was an athletic national champion at a very young age. The training to do this taught me about the dedication and discipline it takes to win.

53. Leaving my ex-husband.

54. No.

55. Crossing the Atlantic in a boat.

56. It was when I took the EST training in the mid-eighties. It was during that seminar that I realized my life is created in my own head and had nothing to do with the circumstances that may surround me.

57. When my husband left me for a man.

58. I had an athletic scholarship in college. Because of an injury, I could not compete at a winning level. I told my coach she should give my scholarship to someone who could help the team win. Her response changed my life, "A team is not only

made up of winners. You're the heart of the team and a leader. That's your role for now."

59. When I married a man who was significantly older than me and had no job, but I knew God had put him in my life for a reason.

60. Not one, but many experiences have molded me. Some build me spiritually and some mentally.

61. Taking charge of my business that had taken me over.

62. When I was sick, my father and other church members came to my bedside and gave me a blessing and prayed for me. I remember almost immediately feeling stronger. The experience convinced me of the power of faith.

63. When my parents divorced and my brother took over caring for me.

64. I damaged a nerve that left me with minimal dexterity in my right arm. Because of it, I could no longer be a surgeon. I found out how intertwined my self-esteem and profession were.

65. When I went to Thailand after a tsunami to help.

66. Calling off my wedding and going for what felt right.

67. Not *a* defining moment, per se, but a culmination and continuation of hundreds of little defining moments.

68. When my husband was in a motorcycle accident.

69. When I joined the Peace Corps after college.

70. Being called to be Relief Society president.

71. No.

72. My defining moment was when I got the principles of the Twelve Steps.

73. No one moment, but my whole upbringing, my friends, my husband, getting laid off from my job, and the birth of my children.

74. When I watched a dear friend deal with cancer. The perspective this put on life for me cannot be put into words.

75. When I was young, I met someone that I talked to on the phone for almost six months before I met him face-to-face. He was African American. We met as people who just talked and bonded; color and gender made no difference. Forty years later we are still friends.

76. When my daughter was born.

77. When, despite all my fears and severe health issues, I took my five children and left an abusive marriage that had made me live in a shell for 15 years.

78. When I discovered energy healing.

79. The day I realized that professionally I am equal to other practitioners. I'd always felt less than them.

80. Overcoming many obstacles.

81. When I learned to fight for what I wanted.

82. It's the sum of all the moments strung together that have made me who I am.

83. When I learned I can choose to be happy and live in the now.

84. Following my father's suicide, I witnessed incredible judgment, anger, loss, fear, greed, assumptions, and just plain ugliness. I've never judged someone again.
85. No.
86. Through experiencing ultimate career highs and then lows, I am a better leader and person.
87. Being named administrative judge without applying for the position.
88. Parenthood made me realize that at some point you just have to let go and trust the Universe. I gained hope and faith.
89. A lot of lessons and mistakes.
90. Are you kidding me? Anyone who answers this question with *one* defining moment is full of shit.
91. Giving birth to my son taught me how to love unconditionally.
92. Being born to my very fascinating and unique parents.
93. My junior year spent in Paris.
94. Learning to never lose myself.
95. Discovering the power of prayer.
96. Getting my PhD taught me how to persevere, never give up, and infused me with sheer determination.
97. I went back to college for eight years when my kids were ages one and four. That made it possible for me to leave my alcoholic husband and take care of my kids on my own.

98. When I walked away from a very lucrative job because I could not be myself in that office.
99. When I chose marriage and children over a career in media.
100. The day I changed who I was and became who I am today. It wasn't a lightning bolt incident, just a day when I sat there and said to myself, *This is it; I am not going to be a weak person any longer.*

4: What Are You Most Proud Of?

1. My children.
2. My ability to stay focused on what's important in my life; hard work, education, physical fitness, family, to care for those who are less fortunate, and to believe in a higher power.
3. The life I have built with my husband.
4. Serving honorably in the US Marines for 22 years as one of the two percent of women represented in the Corps.
5. Overcoming my childhood.
6. That I left an abusive husband with nothing but the clothes on my back.
7. My wonderful son. He is the accomplishment of my life.
8. That I overcame my alcoholism and have created a successful, happy life.
9. Overcoming my limiting beliefs so I could pursue my passion.

10. My personal progress and desire to learn something new every day.
11. My family.
12. Watching my parents rebuild their business, not once but twice.
13. My growth and professional development as a woman in a man's industry.
14. Keeping an open mind and an open heart, even when it is not easy.
15. Raising my children, and now helping with my grandchildren while I'm working full time.
16. Moving to another part of the country with zero support, purely on my conviction that it would lead to a better future for my son and me.
17. My ability to face the things I fear and learn from them.
18. I came from a broken home, spent time in juvenile centers, dropped out of high school, and finished at an alternative school. I am most proud that today I have my master's degree after that very rocky start.
19. My ability to overcome trying situations with my head held high.
20. The life I have created.
21. That I wrote and published a book.
22. Stepping up and being a caregiver to my very ill husband until his last breath. I didn't know I had that kind of courage in me or what an honor it would be.

23. Being open to the clues and puzzle pieces that life gives me. Fitting those pieces together, and then finding amazing discoveries that I would have never thought possible.

24. I'm proud of the many times I have stood up for what is right, even when it had negative consequences.

25. That I got through motherhood! It wasn't easy for me.

26. Overcoming incredible hardships in my life and becoming an inspiration to others.

27. Getting past my anxiety and uncertainty to take on difficult challenges.

28. Overcoming my depression and now living a joy-filled life.

29. My writing and singing.

30. I am proud that all of my children have the Lord and live good lives.

31. That I have helped several women leave abusive relationships.

32. Caring for my elderly parents. I think there is a great deal of honor in that.

33. Helping to raise my stepchildren through the years.

34. My grandchildren.

35. Using the many heartbreaks in my life to become a better person, friend, mother, daughter, sister, and lover.

36. The personal and financial freedom I attained at an early age.

37. Having my kids know how much I love them. My parents didn't know how to give me that.
38. Demonstrating to my daughters how to be strong and independent.
39. I am most proud of the part of my personality that I have cultivated. I chose wisdom over forcefulness. I chose to be passive and compassionate over aggressive and demanding behavior.
40. My two daughters' empathy for others.
41. That I take chances and remain open to new experiences.
42. I'm proud of the times I stood up for people who were too afraid to stand up for themselves.
43. At 21, I have traveled to 11 countries, graduated from college, entered into a master's program, worked at some of the top rehab centers in the world, and become independent from my family.
44. I am proud that I chose enlightenment over the lower consciousness I was raised with.
45. Even through some really hard life experiences, I have been able to find strength to stand up for myself and go on living.
46. That in spite of the harm I have suffered at other's hands, I still have faith, hope, and undying love for people.
47. Being a good wife and mother, which has fulfilled me more than any job ever could.
48. Staying married for over 25 years.

49. The outstanding adults my four children have become. They really went above and beyond to make me proud of them.
50. Starting my own business.
51. The grace and dignity my family has displayed during trying times.
52. The speech I gave at my mom's funeral. It was the most honest and difficult thing that I have ever done in my life. I made myself vulnerable to over 1,000 people.
53. After suffering several serious injuries in an accident, I still completed my college degree on time.
54. Watching my career blossom.
55. I'm proud that, as a nurse, I have cared for hundreds of patients and always gave them the attention and care they needed.
56. On my thirteenth birthday, I wrote in my journal that I wanted to be wise when I grew up. I'm proud of myself for staying true to that, albeit with many side roads taken during the trip.
57. Having a beautiful, healthy family.
58. My personal growth.
59. I am most proud of my parents. They have never been afraid to speak their minds and fight for what they believe in.
60. My husband, who always loves me just as I am.
61. How my family has grown so close.
62. How well my husband and I communicate.
63. My perseverance and loyalty.

64. My daughter. She is the kind and responsible person I always hoped she would be.

65. That I take responsibility for my mistakes and don't blame others.

66. Despite a very difficult adolescence and becoming a teenage mom, I graduated from college *cum laude*.

67. Staying positive and strong.

68. The day I found out I was pregnant with my first child, I quit smoking and have not touched a cigarette since.

69. If my eyes open in the morning, and I get out of bed, I'm proud!

70. That I have made good choices for myself during my lifetime.

71. I am most proud that although I have failed many times, I've never given up.

72. I am successfully managing my home, marriage, children, and a small business while remaining happy.

73. My creative work as an artist.

74. My career, which has changed often, but has always been successful because of my tenacity.

75. Seeing my two daughters go to college.

76. My daughter, who survived cancer at a very young age.

77. My mother. In the seventies, she successfully lobbied to have insurance companies cover reconstructive surgery after breast cancer.

78. Breaking free of the very controlling and conservative religion I was raised in.
79. Being married for 37 years to the man I fell in love with when I was only 15.
80. My children's choices.
81. Being completely content with what I have done with my life.
82. Always helping other people.
83. My ability to assist others on their journey while traveling my own.
84. My ability to take lemons and make lemon pie, lemonade, lemon sorbet, and assorted other lemon-infused recipes for life.
85. My unconventional children. They are wonderful thinkers.
86. Anything I can look back on and say, "Hey! I did that and did it well!"
87. My education. I feel I can learn anything.
88. The many individuals I have helped to find their courage and fly.
89. Achieving success in my career while raising two incredibly well-balanced children.
90. Graduating from college.
91. My independence: personal, intellectual, sexual, and financial.
92. My personality, values, and faith.
93. Pulling myself out of my depression and despair.
94. Giving birth to my son.
95. I am most proud of being different from most people I know.

96. Teaching my children to be true to themselves and to listen to that voice within.
97. Always following my heart.
98. My ability to never stay angry and to forgive.
99. I'm most proud that as a teenager, I never tried drugs.
100. That I lost 60 pounds in just one year, and now I enjoy very good health.

5: Who Influenced You the Most?

1. My grandfather and my mother.
2. My dad. He taught me to value hard work, education, physical fitness. He died when I was 12, but I know that he is a guiding force in every moment of my life.
3. My nanny, the woman who raised me from age six to nine. She was funny and kind and unfailingly patient.
4. My father.
5. My teachers in elementary school.
6. I have influenced myself the most. I am very strong and independent.
7. My husband.
8. My mother, a very smart, strong woman.
9. My parents.
10. By far, my mother. She is the most courageous woman I know. She is incredibly strong and has a heart of gold. I aspire to be like her.
11. My mom.

12. My parents, who were both very hard workers.
13. Writers and poets.
14. My Granna.
15. I think my spiritual studies and changes in my belief system have been my greatest teachers.
16. My aunt has always been and always will be my biggest hero. She has been the solid rock who stood by me through thick and thin. When I didn't believe in myself, she believed in me.
17. My mom and aunt.
18. The memories of my mother's character.
19. My dad, who always gave silent, strong love. He taught me everything has to be right and on time. He never doubted me.
20. I can't point to one person. I have been influenced by good relationships and bad ones, from pain and joy.
21. Gandhi, Edgar Cayce, the Mayans, and many others.
22. My dad, who was a WWII veteran and among the first troops to land on Normandy beach on D-Day. He was a courageous hero.
23. My mom, who always had a positive attitude. She exemplified that courage is leaving the past behind and moving forward. When we lost our home during an economic recession, she just started saving for our next one.
24. My fifth grade teacher, who taught me a love for learning.

25. My boss of 20 years. She believes that leadership is love. Good leaders not only love what they do, they love their people.
26. My grandmother, who taught me to just trust God and know that I'm always beautiful and talented.
27. My husband and daughter.
28. Some people have influenced me by my *not* wanting to be like them, and others by my wanting to be like them. I try to emulate the best and learn from both.
29. My grandparents.
30. God.
31. I grew up with a single mom who had bipolar issues that went untreated. I would watch the mistakes she would make and be determined to not do the same.
32. I think I've influenced myself the most. My father was an alcoholic, and my mother didn't know how to stand up for herself, and I grew up from their mistakes.
33. My mom, who taught me to never, never, never give up!
34. My grandmother. She was deeply religious, kind, funny, and generous. She left anyone who came in contact with her feeling special and loved— especially me.
35. My father was an ex-convict who fell into fighting and poverty over and over. Surprisingly, he taught me that no matter how flawed a person is love can transform them.

36. Positively, my grandmother's humility. Negatively, the Catholic Church.

37. My mom, the most unselfish, caring, and strong woman I have ever known. She always pushed our family to take control of their own lives.

38. Confident and strong-willed friends that I have met over time.

39. My fearless therapist, who taught me that when it comes to feelings, "The only way out is through," and "What you resist, persists."

40. My second grade teacher, who praised my writing skills and set me on the path to my life's work.

41. My mom, who projected all her splendid gifts onto me; profound intuition, a way with words, and uncanny strength.

42. There is not one particular person. I took bits and pieces from many of my friends and colleagues who were women balancing marriage, children, and career.

43. My mother, who made me feel like I could accomplish anything I wanted to take on.

44. My grandmother, who never hesitated to stand up for her beliefs no matter who she was with.

45. My inner Self.

46. My parents, whom I miss very much.

47. My husband.

48. My mother, who died in a tragic event. When people are gone, you remember their best.

49. My father, who took me away from my abusive marriage.

50. My father, who taught me to see the humor in absolutely everything.
51. My gymnastics coach. She was a perfect role model.
52. Sunny Dawn Johnston and Oprah.
53. My parents and their characters.
54. My mother. She always held up during hard times and tried to not let them affect her kids. Now that I'm a mother, I appreciate how hard that is.
55. My therapist.
56. For better and for worse, my mom.
57. LDS President Gordon B. Hinkley.
58. My grandfather. My father was not around at all until I was a teenager, and my grandfather filled his role and taught me about being responsible and taking care of myself.
59. People who take the initiative to use their time and resources to help others.
60. I didn't have great role models growing up, so I tended to look for female role models in public figures like musicians and actresses. Chrissie Hind, Alice Bag, Lydia Lunch, and Exene Cervenka were all women who were brave, intelligent, and not at all concerned with traditional ideas about how a woman should act, dress, or talk.
61. My soccer moms.
62. Rosemary, a woman who is about my mother's age. She's taught me that life should always be about learning, and I should continue to live my dreams even when I'm old.

63. Since I am only mildly ambitious, I am constantly inspired by self-made women who make it big, like Barbara Corcoran, J. K. Rowling, Oprah, Martha Stewart, etc.

64. My mother, who by being abused by men taught me that I do not have to do the same thing.

65. Other creative women who dare.

66. My grandparents, who taught me how to save money.

67. Several of my high school teachers and college professors.

68. Society has influenced me greatly, because I wanted to "show them all" that a young woman from a broken home could have a great career, a great family, and a great life.

69. One of my uncles, who loved me when I didn't feel lovable at all.

70. My Al-Anon sponsor, who gives me strength and hope during and after our meetings.

71. At different times, I've felt equal influence from my husband, children, family, and friends.

72. The women in my family.

73. There was never a big, influential person in my life. Rather, a series of little shifts, little messages that just came along at just the right time through a song on the radio, a line in a book, or just the right person on my path.

74. My maternal grandmother, who allowed me to be a child. I was the oldest of five children, and

my mother put a lot of responsibility on me with housework and babysitting.

75. My eldest child. Prior to his birth, I was on a self-destructive course. The moment I realized that I was responsible for another being and that I was their greatest example, I knew it was time to conduct myself differently.

76. The women leaders in my church.

77. My college friends.

78. Anyone who doesn't take no for an answer.

79. My children, who both softened and toughened me up.

80. My mother. She was always ahead of her time, which made her very unpopular.

81. Authors such as Joel Osteen, Rhonda Byrne, Carolyn Cooper, Marianne Williamson, Marnie Pehrson, and Rhonda Hess.

82. People with much more experience than I have as well as some of my direct reports who provide me with *aha* moments.

83. Close childhood friends.

84. Me, me, me, me, me, meeeeeeeeeeee (please sing this answer as if an operatic scale).

85. My law partners.

86. My parents with their simple truths, faith, and unconditional love.

87. There have been a lot of people who influenced me, but I believe the one who influenced me the most was *me*! Because it is me who decides what

feels right or wrong and then makes the outside match the inside in all things.

88. My husband, for his support and belief in my abilities.

89. At work, brilliant women who inspire me.

90. Smart, strong outspoken women like Jane Fonda, Golda Meier, Hillary Clinton, and Michelle Obama.

91. My close girlfriends.

92. I have had many spiritual teachers along life's path, but my greatest influences are all the real life experiences I have had through the people I love.

93. This would have to be a prior coworker who guided me through many of my life's most difficult times. I don't think she even knew how much of an influence she had on me.

94. Critical thinkers like my sister.

95. Other women who do things I admire and who are not afraid to go *big*!

96. My parents.

97. The writings of Wayne Dyer.

98. My mother-in-law, a model of grace and strength.

99. All of my strong girlfriends who held me up when I thought I was going down.

100. Everyone I meet influences me.

6: If You Could Live Your Life Again, What One Thing Would You Change?

1. I don't believe in looking back. Everything that has happened to me has made me who I am, and I like myself!
2. I would be quicker to forgive.
3. I would not lose touch with so many people I have loved.
4. I would be a better daughter to my mother.
5. I would be faster to move forward after hard times.
6. I would develop myself spiritually at a younger age.
7. I would forget about boys and study more.
8. I wouldn't change even one thing.
9. I would not waste time worrying about things I cannot change.
10. I would enjoy how much I matter to the people who love me more.
11. I would finish college.
12. I would not change even one thing.
13. I would seek professional help for my emotional eating and body image issues.
14. I would relive the moments I made myself unavailable to my loved ones and do that differently.
15. I would change the way I reacted in certain situations, not knowing I had control over how I felt.

16. At a younger age, I would know that every experience, bad or good, teaches me something.
17. I would work harder to create a closer, tight-knit family.
18. Nothing.
19. I would be more respectful and loving toward my parents.
20. The moments I have used my influence to hurt others.
21. I wish now I had followed my dream to become an interior designer.
22. I would have not tried to be perfect for everyone else.
23. I would have been more open to feedback from others and been quicker to act on it.
24. Enlisting the help of women mentors, both professionally and personally.
25. I think I have lived the life I was meant to live.
26. I would meet my second husband much sooner.
27. I would follow my dreams rather than allowing others to discourage me.
28. Nothing.
29. I would change my childhood to one in which I had a loving family.
30. I would become a doctor or a nurse.
31. I would do my best at everything I tried and not be afraid to lose or look silly.
32. I would have made my education a higher priority.
33. I'm where I'm supposed to be, right here, right now.

34. I would tell myself to not worry so much about the people who hurt, used, or did not appreciate me.
35. I would focus more on my family and the other people I love.
36. I would have started a family after I finished my education.
37. I'd zoom in on that DNA strand that caused my son's mental illness and realign the molecules so he'd have a life of joy instead of suffering.
38. I would make everything less about me.
39. I would pay more attention to those moments that made me a more thoughtful, caring human being.
40. I would have taken my family to live abroad for a couple of years so they could experience a different culture.
41. I would not attempt to fix everyone else, only myself.
42. I would not have been as indulgent with my children, which would have made them more independent.
43. I wouldn't be such an enabler.
44. My ability to have more children.
45. Nothing.
46. I am so proud of who I've become, I would not change a thing.
47. I would not have given up so quickly on my marriage.
48. I had so much athletic success in my youth, I think I may have an inflated sense of entitlement.

49. I would have invested my earnings in property in South Africa.
50. I would not choose a college major based on its likelihood of getting me a job. I studied accounting and then hated my job for 30 years.
51. I would have fought harder to get into the Coast Guard.
52. Nothing.
53. This is my life's story; I would not change a word of it.
54. I would have followed my gut earlier.
55. Enjoy everything more, especially my kids.
56. Prevent my ex-husband from damaging our older kids.
57. I wish I could have found a way to take addiction out of this world.
58. I wouldn't change anything. Everything happened for a reason and made me who I am.
59. I would try to be less self-centered in my twenties and thirties.
60. I could say, "If only I had not married that man," but then I wouldn't have my kids.
61. I would never, ever take abuse from anyone.
62. I would not have taken the attitude of "I'll figure it out later," so often.
63. I would pursue a career in a field that I love.
64. I would not have gotten married so young.
65. I would have played more.
66. I would take better care of my body earlier in life.
67. I would have gotten a business degree.

68. If I had known about ALANON, I would have gone as a teen. I suffered needlessly because I found it late in life.
69. I wish I could have balanced the discipline and high expectations I was brought up with, with more love and happiness.
70. I'd have more children.
71. Not marry my first husband.
72. I would remove the sexual abuse I experienced as a child.
73. I would be tougher with my children when they were teenagers. I had strict limits when they were little, but when they became teens I wanted them to like me.
74. I would not have been sexually abused throughout many years of my life.
75. The only thing I would change is discovering much younger that surviving awful experiences makes me strong.
76. I don't think I would change anything.
77. I would have taken relationships with men more seriously and settled down earlier.
78. Be more true to myself and not try to please others so much.
79. I would have loved to be more confident in myself when I was young.
80. At a much younger age, I would know my worth and walk with power and purpose.
81. I would not be so afraid to fail.

82. I would like to have been a teacher. I think I would be a great one.
83. I would start doing yoga much earlier in my life.
84. I would continue to work part-time while my children were young.
85. Learn earlier in life not to be selfish.
86. Love myself more and sooner.
87. After law school, I wish I had gone into the public sector rather than a law firm.
88. Nothing.
89. At first I could think of many things I would change, but then I realized that I benefited from each of those things.
90. It would have been nice to start my business the right way the first time, rather than the tough lessons of doing it wrong many times!
91. I would have praised my children more.
92. I wish I could have understood myself the way I do now 20 years ago.
93. I wish I had taken more electives in school to broaden my education.
94. I would read more. Especially the classics.
95. I would love myself more.
96. I wouldn't change anything. I've loved my life, mistakes and all!
97. I would have worked harder and played less. I feel I could have made so much more of myself.
98. I would have gotten to know my parents better as people.

99. Nothing.
100. I would have lived in the moment more often.

7: What Do You Want Your Legacy to Be?

1. To have left many people a little better than I found them.
2. Core values in my children of caring for those less fortunate than themselves.
3. I want to leave a legacy that will change healthcare for all of humanity. I want everyone to know they deserve to be healed in mind, body, and spirit.
4. I hope that people will say I was nice.
5. I want my children to be happy, productive, self-sufficient, and healthy throughout their lives.
6. I want to be remembered as a leader in my community who made a difference in the lives of children and families.
7. I hope that the world is a better place because of my commitments of time and money.
8. I want to have had an impact on repairing the world.
9. I want the people I have interacted with to know that relationships are everything.
10. Love rules all.
11. See the magic all around you in every moment.
12. I want to leave children and grandchildren who are happy and love life.
13. No matter what I went through, I was strong, happy, and stayed encouraged.

14. I want people to smile when they think of me!
15. I want to be remembered as a caring and nurturing mother, understanding friend, and loving wife.
16. My legacy will be the knowledge for healing I have been divinely blessed with.
17. I want my legacy to be one of integrity, awareness, perseverance, empathy, service, and strength.
18. That I tried to treat others as I would like to be treated. That golden rule is my mantra.
19. I hope I have been one of those people in others' paths with a lesson just at the moment it was needed.
20. That I said or did something that influenced or touched a life.
21. I hope that I inspired new points of view that opened up new possibilities for people.
22. I want to leave a legacy of kindness.
23. I have taught my children to be good people who do not judge others, even if they are difficult. But they never need to put up with abuse.
24. Love and happiness.
25. That happiness and peaceful living are here for all of us, even if it comes and goes.
26. *Carpe diem.*
27. I want to be remembered with joy and laughter.
28. I want everyone who walked my journey with me to know that I loved them.
29. I want my daughters to be loaded with confidence.

30. I want to write books that bring comfort and happiness into the lives of others.
31. That I was able to give my children the encouragement and security they needed to become positive adults.
32. I would like to be thought of as an honest person who did her best to support and care for others.
33. I want to be remembered for helping my children and friends.
34. I want my legacy to be that I was a genuinely good person.
35. Reflecting the light of Christ, even just by smiling and saying hello.
36. Honesty and integrity.
37. That it is possible to create a great relationship where you have openness, honesty, love, connection, and fun.
38. That I never threw in the towel!
39. I would like to give this world love.
40. If you are going to do something, do it with joy.
41. That I was a woman of faith and had a very kind heart, always wanting to help others.
42. Where there is laughter, there is love.
43. That I loved to cook and feed people.
44. I want the people I've loved to know that.
45. How important family support is.
46. That I was kind, fair, and true to myself.
47. That I've always stood up for what I believe to be right.
48. That I have loved and been loved.

49. In spite of the challenges I've faced, that I've lived life to the fullest.
50. The lives I have touched as an educator.
51. I want my children to know their mother and father worked hard to make a good life for them, and that they will do the same for their children.
52. That people felt loved and appreciated when they were with me.
53. I want to be remembered as someone who was kind and encouraged people.
54. Love, service, and a body of literature conveying the message that our human lives are sacred, and all is well.
55. I want to let all women know that God made us very courageous and powerful beings.
56. Don't be afraid to try, and try again.
57. I want to leave people knowing that everyone has a purpose.
58. I want people to know that I helped them to be happier and to laugh at some point in their lives.
59. I want to leave a legacy of calm, compassionate, limitless love.
60. Love, compassion, strength, and fun.
61. That I was always there for whomever needed me.
62. I want people to remember me as a good person.
63. Being a wonderful mother, wife, and educator.
64. That I had so many reasons to give up, but I picked myself up and lived life the best I could.
65. That my family knows I have loved them just as they are.

66. Live in joy!
67. I want to inspire others to have the courage to *be*!
68. I want to be remembered as helping everyone I meet to claim their brilliance and feel confident and happy with the amazing opportunities they are offered.
69. To leave this world a better place than when I arrived.
70. That my findings will enlighten the thought processes of everyone.
71. I want to be an example of acceptance, giving, receiving, questioning, and growing.
72. A love and excitement for nature.
73. Love and laughter.
74. That people will look back and see all the great things I did, knowing that I went through a lot of really hard times, but was able to stay strong and positive.
75. My heart led me.
76. That I did not judge others from my own point of view.
77. I want to leave books and programs that will benefit women the world over.
78. That I made people feel good through humor.
79. That I was a hard worker and always willing to go the extra mile.
80. That I truly loved and cared for my family and friends.
81. I hope people know how much I loved them and that I had a good life.

82. The legacy of self-love.
83. The strength to do what is right.
84. Transformed lives of better health and emotional intelligence.
85. Sustainable fishing in global communities.
86. My mission is to help people find parts of themselves that they love and find ways to use those parts to serve themselves and others.
87. To have been a role model for my children of fun, hard work, and grace.
88. For my niece and nephew to know how much I love them and want to be a guiding force in their lives.
89. To love and cherish God as my Lord and Savior.
90. That I was a loving mother.
91. That I was a strong and loving leader who proudly served my country.
92. That I helped other women on my way up.
93. That I could make people laugh.
94. That I inspired people to stop and think.
95. My healthy, beautiful family.
96. That I was kind and treaded lightly.
97. That whatever I did, I did it with love in my heart.
98. I hope people remember me for how I helped them understand and appreciate themselves better.
99. I was always careful with criticism.
100. That I brought comfort and happiness to many lives.

8: What Do You Want Other Women to Know?

1. I want their success and happiness as much as my own.
2. Live each day to the fullest and love unconditionally.
3. Find your voice and believe in yourself.
4. Know your own self-worth, and own your spirit.
5. Know you are not alone.
6. Reach out and find good people to support you and value those people forever.
7. *Cosmopolitan* magazine is written by idiots. Also, people with money, taste, and good sense do not buy shoes that cost $1,900.
8. Embrace every moment of being a woman. We have the intuition to love strongly and bring balance to our family and friends.
9. Do not limit yourself by the stories you make up about why you can't pursue your dreams.
10. Other women are not the enemy.
11. Good friends that are women are the best things you can have. I have longed for, and missed, my women friends more than any man.
12. We have the right to be happy and live our lives fully.
13. Believe in yourself.
14. Life is a journey, not a race. Pace yourself.
15. Laugh at yourself whenever you can.
16. Be strong and stick together.

17. There is always a way, you just have to be tenacious enough to find it.
18. We are perfect exactly as we are. Be loud and proud of ourselves, for it is all we have!
19. The only thing to be aware of is what and who we are, and that we remain true to our own self.
20. No matter what, life keeps going, and we can either sit and let past situations beat us down, or move forward and create the life we want.
21. It is most important for a woman to respect herself and try to live with grace.
22. Make your own decisions, no matter what advice others give you.
23. Let other people help you.
24. Give it your all, even if you fail.
25. Change is good, even if it isn't your idea.
26. Keep searching, growing, learning.
27. Never give up any part of yourself for a man.
28. Be kind to one another.
29. You are the most powerful person in your universe.
30. Think for yourself.
31. Everyone has the potential to be great.
32. Find meaningful and productive ways to express the gifts God has given you.
33. Your voice *does* matter.
34. We are all in this together.
35. Have fun, and celebrate each day.
36. We each can be and do anything.

37. Stop spending money on clothing and small, crappy things. Save it and experience security.
38. Don't let anyone tell you that you have to get married and have children in order to be happy.
39. Don't worry so much about the future.
40. Just keep on trucking.
41. Only you get to decide how amazing or how terrible your own life can be.
42. There is always a lesson to be learned and something positive in every situation.
43. I love them all, just as they are.
44. You are capable.
45. Even if they've been dealt a tough hand, it doesn't mean that the whole deck is stacked against them.
46. Listen to your children.
47. Read, read, read. Then read something that doesn't agree with your point of view.
48. I want women to know that we are the backbone of society. We are strong fighters and winners.
49. There are no expectations you should feel compelled to meet, except your own.
50. We do not have to be obedient.
51. Nothing in life worth having ever comes easily.
52. Never settle—if you want something, go out and get it.
53. It takes lots of failures before success comes.
54. I want women to know that they are all gorgeous just the way God made them.

55. With every decision you make, remember you are the role model for the next generation of women.
56. If women could get along, we could conquer the world!
57. Whether it be work, family, or community, we need to learn how to support each other's best.
58. You can make your marriage good. Work at it.
59. Take care of yourself. You do matter.
60. Find your passion and do it.
61. All you have to do is live your life to the fullest and be true to yourself.
62. Every woman is so much stronger than she realizes.
63. Our low points do not define us. Never get stuck in them.
64. Celebrate who you are and do things that will make you proud of yourself.
65. We have been blessed with the ability to love unconditionally because we are mothers.
66. Working together, we can accomplish anything.
67. I want women to know that I am always there for them.
68. We deserve to be treated with respect.
69. I wish every woman would know that she has done well.
70. Be kind to yourself.
71. We are all one, with the same loves, fears, and desires.
72. Women rule this world; the men just don't know it yet.

73. Empathy and kindness reaches across any aisle.
74. The harder something is to achieve, the more you'll appreciate it once you've done it.
75. The hard part of "You can do anything you want to," is knowing what you want.
76. Life is so much better when you follow your instincts.
77. Do a soul search, and define your priorities.
78. No matter what you go through, get out of bed in the morning, and go do something for someone else.
79. The happy times always outweigh the bad ones.
80. You will be most at peace when you find balance between your spiritual life, family, work, and exercise.
81. If a decision you are faced with causes harm to others, there is probably a better choice.
82. You can't be good for anyone else until you are good to yourself.
83. Do what is best for *you*!
84. The world needs you to be exactly who you are.
85. Don't play small—you have greatness within you.
86. If it hurts you to leave your children in the care of someone else, don't do it.
87. Confidence is imperative.
88. Enjoy all the chapters of your life—it will make a great book someday!
89. It's okay, even good, to lean and be leaned on.
90. Trust yourself and your instincts.

91. Always stay in the now and find lots to be grateful for.
92. There is no one right path.
93. Be willing to ask for and receive help—life is not meant to be endured alone.
94. Don't be slow to right the mistakes you've made.
95. Take good care of yourself so you can take care of others without resentment.
96. When you speak, speak to be heard...but remember that tone and timing are everything.
97. Always count your blessings.
98. Love yourself unconditionally.
99. Never neglect the little girl inside you. Never stop learning, laughing, or discovering the magic around you and the majesty inside you.
100. Women *rock*!

About the Author

Terry Sidford has been a certified life coach for the past 15 years and has assisted scores of people in achieving their dreams, which she believes is her own life's purpose. Terry's greatest joy has always been to help others unleash their potential and live life to the fullest. Based on her success as a life coach, she has been asked to speak at many personal growth and business-related events. Terry also authors a widely acclaimed newsletter that focuses on her principles of *Being*. She was professionally trained by The Coaches Training Institute and received an Associate Certified Coach credential from the International Coaching Federation.

To add to her diverse background, Terry trained at Body Balance University and National Exercise and Sports Trainer Association to become a certified Pilates instructor. Since then, she's taught Pilates for the past nine years. In addition, she is a licensed real estate agent in Utah.

Terry was raised in Southern California and has lived in Utah for more than 30 years. She's active in the outdoors, plays tennis, runs, and skis. Currently she resides in Park City with her husband, Matthew, and has two sons, Alex and Connor.

CPSIA information can be obtained
at www.ICGtesting.com
Printed in the USA
FSOW01n1423280815
10395FS